D1251179

The Critical Idiom

General Editor: JOHN D. JUMP

32   *Modern Verse Drama*

In the same series

Tragedy *Clifford Leech*
Romanticism *Lilian R. Furst*
Aestheticism *R. V. Johnson*
The Conceit *K. K. Ruthven*
The Absurd *Arnold P. Hinchliffe*
Fancy and Imagination *R. L. Brett*
Satire *Arthur Pollard*
Metre, Rhyme and Free Verse *G. S. Fraser*
Realism *Damian Grant*
The Romance *Gillian Beer*
Drama and the Dramatics *S. W. Dawson*
Plot *Elizabeth Dipple*
Irony *D. C. Muecke*
Allegory *John MacQueen*
Pastoral *P. V. Marinelli*
Symbolism *Charles Chadwick*
The Epic *Paul Merchant*
Naturalism *Lilian R. Furst and Peter N. Skrine*
Rhetoric *Peter Dixon*
Primitivism *Michael Bell*
Comedy *Moelwyn Merchant*
Burlesque *John D. Jump*
Dada and Surrealism *C. W. E. Bigsby*
The Grotesque *Philip Thomson*
Metaphor *Terence Hawkes*
The Sonnet *John Fuller*
Classicism *Dominique Secretan*
Melodrama *James Smith*
Expressionism *R. S. Furness*
The Ode *John D. Jump*
Myth *K. K. Ruthven*
The Picaresque *Harry Sieber*
Biography *Alan Shelston*
The Stanza *Ernst Häublein*

Modern Verse Drama/
Arnold P. Hinchliffe

Methuen & Co Ltd

First published 1977
by Methuen & Co Ltd
11 New Fetter Lane London EC4P 4EE
© 1977 Arnold P. Hinchliffe

Printed in Great Britain by
Fletcher & Son Ltd., Norwich
Bound by Richard Clay (The Chaucer Press) Ltd
Bungay, Suffolk

ISBN 0416 83250 4 Hardback
ISBN 0416 83260 1 Paperback

Distributed in the USA by
HARPER & ROW PUBLISHERS INC
BARNES & NOBLE IMPORT DIVISION

for GIOVANNI

When it comes to the present age, we are not going to be deterred by a fatalistic philosophy of history from wanting a poetic drama, and from believing that there must be some way of getting it. Besides, the craving for poetic drama is permanent in human nature.

T. S. Eliot

Contents

General Editor's Preface		ix
Foreword		xi
Acknowledgements		xiii
1	Modern Verse Drama	1
2	Poets in the Theatre	15
3	Religious Verse Drama	32
4	T. S. Eliot	37
5	Christopher Fry	53
6	Poets of the Theatre	64
7	Poetic Drama	73
	Bibliography	77
	Index	79

General Editor's Preface

The volumes composing the Critical Idiom deal with a wide variety of key terms in our critical vocabulary. The purpose of the series differs from that served by the standard glossaries of literary terms. Many terms are adequately defined for the needs of students by the brief entries in these glossaries, and such terms do not call for attention in the present series. But there are other terms which cannot be made familiar by means of compact definitions. Students need to grow accustomed to them through simple and straightforward but reasonably full discussions. The main purpose of this series is to provide such discussions.

Many critics have borrowed methods and criteria from currently influential bodies of knowledge or belief that have developed without particular reference to literature. In our own century, some of them have drawn on art, history, psychology, or sociology. Others, strong in a comprehensive faith, have looked at literature and literary criticism from a Marxist or a Christian or some other sharply defined point of view. The result has been the importation into literary criticism of terms from the vocabularies of these sciences and creeds. Discussions of such bodies of knowledge and belief in their bearing upon literature and literary criticism form a natural extension of the initial aim of the Critical Idiom.

Because of their diversity of subject-matter, the studies in the series vary considerably in structure. But all authors have tried to give as full illustrative quotation as possible, to make reference whenever appropriate to more than one literature, and to write in such a way as to guide readers towards the short bibliographies in which they have made suggestions for further reading.

John D. Jump

University of Manchester

Foreword

This brief study is in no way intended to replace, or compete with, Denis Donoghue's work on modern verse drama, *The Third Voice*, but it did start with a doubt raised by that work. It seemed to me that the chapter on Christopher Fry while sober and accurate in terms of drama was less than fair in terms of theatre, and even verse drama should struggle towards existence in that impure space called the stage. In fact the book which proved most useful to this study was George Steiner's *The Death of Tragedy* which, in spite of its title and subject, comes nearer the problems of verse in our modern theatre than Donoghue's work.

The study has been a fascinating journey involving drama and theatre in a very wide way, but I have tried to resist the interesting side-tracks as far as possible. Of course it could be argued that verse drama in these days is only a cul-de-sac and that to treat it seriously at all requires faith in spite of the facts. The value of verse in the modern theatre is certainly doubtful, and must be strenuously maintained or unscrupulously redefined. Fortunately, in a history, faith and fact can often live happily together and particularly when it becomes clear that verse drama was not a cul-de-sac, but rather a long way round, with picturesque scenes on the way.

Arnold P. Hinchliffe

Manchester, 1974

Acknowledgements

I must thank Janice Price and my editor, the late John Jump, for the enthusiasm and support which converted an idea into a labour which proved to rewarding; and Mrs Thelma Wright for typing the final version. Acknowledgements are also due to the following for permission to reprint material from published works: from *The Ascent of F6* by W. H. Auden and Christopher Isherwood, Faber & Faber Ltd and Random House Inc; from *Leonardo's Last Supper* by Peter Barnes, Heinemann Educational Books Ltd; from *Waiting for Godot* by Samuel Beckett, Faber & Faber Ltd and Grove Press Inc; from *Brecht on Theatre* translated by John Willett, Methuen & Co Ltd and Farrer, Strauss and Giroux Inc; from *The Empty Space* by Peter Brook, MacGibbon & Kee Ltd; from 'The Art of the Theatre' by E. Gordon Craig, in *The Theory of the Modern Stage* ed. Eric Bentley, Heinemann Educational Books Ltd; from *The Third Voice* by Denis Donoghue, Princeton University Press; from *Murder in the Cathedral, The Cocktail Party* and *The Elder Statesman* by T. S. Eliot, Faber & Faber Ltd and Harcourt Brace Jovanovitch Inc; from *Brief Chronicles* by Martin Esslin, Maurice Temple Smith Ltd; from *Experimental Theatre* by James Roose-Evans, Studio Vista Ltd and Universe Books; from *The Firstborn, A Phoenix Too Frequent, The Lady's Not For Burning, The Dark is Light Enough* and *Curtmantle* by Christopher Fry, Oxford University Press Ltd; from *Selected Letters and Speeches* by Henrik Ibsen, ed. Evert Sprinchorn, MacGibbon & Kee Ltd; from *Home* by David Storey, Jonathan Cape; from *Anger and After* by John Russell Taylor, Methuen & Co Ltd and Farrar, Strauss and Giroux Inc; from *Cranmer* by Charles Williams, in *The Collected Plays*, Oxford University Press Ltd.

I

Modern Verse Drama

A large question mark hangs over the title. Clearly 'modern' can mean anything according to its context (try asking an ancient historian what he means by modern!) but here, for the purposes of argument, it means something that happened in the British Theatre in the 1930s and 1940s which seems crucial in the larger struggles of verse drama. Even that word 'drama' which seems so solid has its elusive quality which may sound surprising until one thinks about the list in *The Art of Drama* which runs from *Agamemnon* to *The Playboy of the Western World* and leads the author, Ronald Peacock, to suggest that the voice of the dramatist is so individual that 'the association in a form known as drama seems fortuitous and of little consequence' (p. 102). And when we turn to verse the difficulties intensify. Criticism suffers from too many terms and too much confusion about them. We have prose, verse and poetry and we can usually distinguish prose from verse but this leaves us asking what we mean by poetry. It is not a modern question. Aristotle, in *Poetics*, noted that Homer and Empedocles were both called poets though they have nothing in common except their metre: 'the former, therefore, justly merits the name of poet; while the other should rather be called a physiologist than a poet.' (Everyman edition, translated Thomas Twining, p. 6). There was no real urgency to the problem while verse served a common purpose until the nineteenth century when the Romantic movement defined a specialized idea of poetry. This helped the growing recognition that many works obviously in prose were producing results usually associated with poetry. For Aristotle tragedy was in verse because verse was the natural form and the iambic metre 'the most colloquial; as appears evidently from this fact, that our common conversation frequently falls into iambic verse; seldom into hexameter, and only when we depart from our usual melody of speech.' (ibid., pp. 11–12).

But what happens when conversation does not fall naturally into iambics? In the twentieth century some dramatists have confused us by returning to unnatural verse in an age of prose, an age when prose has, moreover, absorbed the techniques of poetry if not verse.

So: we have too many terms. Denis Donoghue, in *The Third Voice*, begins *his* study of modern verse drama with 'poetic drama', 'verse drama', 'prose drama', 'dramatic verse' and 'dramatic poetry' and attempts a distinction, on page 3, between poetic drama and verse drama. He points out that T. S. Eliot seems to make the two terms synonymous – which may explain those critics who have been able to describe his plays as poetic, written in prose printed as verse. In fact Donoghue sees verse drama as a 'purely technical phrase':

it makes no implications whatever as to the quality of the script or of the play as a whole. Unlike 'poetic drama', it is entirely neutral in its application.

This may or may not be so: critical terms are never so passionately used as when they claim neutrality. We must admit, however, that Mr Donoghue is correct when he writes that it is customary 'and appropriate' to describe plays by Ibsen, Shaw and Synge, which are clearly not verse drama, as 'poetic dramas'. And they are clearly not in verse because verse, as John Arden puts it:

is an arrangement of ideas in metrical form with or without

rhyme and similar devices, which generally involves more than one principal meaning. In other words, we use the associations of words and images as strengthened by our metre and rhyme to remind us of an almost unlimited range of associations over and beyond their surface significance; in prose, however, each word simply means what it says and nothing else.

> (Speech to NUS Drama Festival in Leeds, printed in
> New Theatre Magazine, vol. 11, 3 April 1961)

This last sentence concerning prose is unfortunate, but it reminds us that our present debate between poetic and verse drama was, initially, a debate on the relative merits of verse and prose. George Steiner, in chapter VII of his illuminating study *The Death of Tragedy*, recalls that for two thousand years the notion of tragic drama and verse had been inseparable, that verse imposes on the mind a sense of occasion, that its form is memorable (literally so; witness its use in television advertising). As the medium which divides the world of high tragedy from that of ordinary existence verse simplifies and complicates. It simplifies because it strips away the problems of material contingency: as Steiner briskly observes, bathrooms only exist in tragedy for Agamemnon to be murdered in. So verse does not express menial facts, or, for that matter, comedy and in modern verse drama it has been required to do both. No, verse matches the actors who wore high shoes and spoke through great masks, characters who lived, spoke and thought higher and louder than life.

Yet the theatre in England has seldom been pure. Shakespeare, we know, uses prose and verse as character, circumstance or mood demand, though he was usually conventional about those demands, retaining prose for peasants and comedy. The audience of the time was used to verse and considered an elevated style natural for character of noble birth and yet we find Corneille writing in the Examen to *Andromède* (1650):

J'avoue que les vers que l'on récite sur le théâtre sont présumés être prose; nous ne parlons pas d'ordinaire en vers et sans cette fiction leur mesure et leur rime sortiraient du vraisemblable ...

(I assume that the verse spoken in the theatre is supposed to be prose; we do not ordinarily speak in verse and without this assumption the metre and rhyme will depart from the truth ...)

Writers like Fontenelle and La Motte protested against the tyranny of verse and in 1722 La Motte began to write prose tragedies though he lacked the talent to suggest the possible strength of the medium. The argument, therefore, is not recent and Donoghue devotes his first chapter to a 'neutral survey' of this problem ranging from La Motte through Stendhal (who repeatedly declared during the 1820s that tragedy could only survive in prose), Ibsen and William Archer to statements by recent poets and critics like Yvor Winters who found verse dead for drama. The problem is one of naturalness. Aristotle may maintain that conversation lapses naturally into iambic metres but subsequent generations spoke differently. How could verse with its rhythm, syntax and diction be related to the common language of the audience to which it was addressed, and Donoghue quotes from Cinthio, Castelvetro, Corneille, Dryden and Victor Hugo arguing for their own beliefs and proving nothing.

For we must remember that drama, unlike the lyric, is not primarily a verbal composition: the words emerge from the underlying structure of incident and character. Aristotle pointed out that the poet (or 'maker') should be a maker of plots rather than of verses since he is a poet because he imitates and what he imitates are actions. Which leads us to another confusion of words: between drama and theatre.

Let us first tackle the central problem of verse and prose which was brought to a head in the theatre by one man: Ibsen. Here, however, we have other problems. We must decide what Ibsen did, what people said Ibsen had done and what the consequences were of both. And what, in the larger perspective, did it all mean. Ibsen's views on verse drama are conveniently summed up in his famous letter to Lucie Wolf who had asked him to write a prologue for her:

> The prologue would of course have to be in verse, since that is the established custom. But I will take no part in perpetuating this custom. Verse has been most injurious to the art of drama. A true artist of the stage, whose repertoire is the contemporary drama, should not be willing to let a single verse cross her lips. It is improbable that verse will be employed to any extent worth mentioning in the drama of the immediate future since the aims of the dramatists of the future are almost certain to be incompatible with it ... During the last seven or eight years I have hardly written a single verse, devoting myself exclusively to the very much more difficult art of writing the straightforward, plain language spoken in real life.
>
> (*Selected Letters*, 25 May 1883, pp. 217–18)

Ibsen's struggle towards that 'very much more difficult art' was neither brief nor simple and it has been exhaustively traced by Michael Meyer whose *abridged* version of *Ibsen* in Penguin Books runs to over 900 pages. Ibsen had an extraordinary facility for writing verse, especially rhymed verse, in any metre and he made his break slowly and deliberately. Prose was the medium natural to the action he sought to portray and this implies a break with the kind of action and the kind of actor in the theatre of his time. To that theatre comedy might be in prose but tragedy must be in verse, and the notion that tragedy could be about ordinary people speaking the language of the streets would have struck both the actors and the audience as absurd. Ibsen at first restricted prose to peasants and lower-class characters but in *The Pretenders* (1863) there are signs of an attempt to create a living, colloquial language. Meyer claims the line – 'Buy a dog, my lord' – as the beginning of modern prose drama (*Ibsen*, pp. 221–2). *The League of Youth* (1869) was Ibsen's first attempt to write a play entirely in modern colloquial dialogue dealing with the 'forces and frictions in modern life' (letter to Hegel, October 1868, *Selected Letters*, p. 75) and written in prose 'which gives it a strong realistic colouring' (letter to Georg Brandes, *Selected Letters*, p. 84). As William Archer pointed out Ibsen's criticism of life needed to come to closer terms with reality 'and to that end he required a suppler instrument than verse' (quoted Meyer, pp. 311–12). It was not easy for one to whom verse came easily to abandon a medium in which he felt free for one which constricted him but, as he wrote in a letter to Fru Heiberg – which was in verse: prose is for ideas, verse for visions. After the epics *Brand* (1866) and *Peer Gynt* (1867) which established his reputation as a verse dramatist he wrote his next epic, *Emperor and Galilean* (1873), in prose, a decision he defended in a letter to Edmund Gosse dated 15 January 1874:

> You say the drama ought to have been written in verse and that it would have gained by this. Here I must differ from you. As you must have observed, the play is conceived in the most realistic style. The illusion I wished to produce was that of reality. I wished to produce the impression on the reader that what he was reading was something that had actually happened. If I had employed verse, I would have counteracted my own intention and defeated my purpose. The many ordinary, insignificant characters whom I have intentionally introduced into the play would have become indistinct and indistinguishable from one another if I had allowed all of them to speak in the same metre. We are no longer living in the days of Shakespeare ... Speaking generally, the dialogue must conform to the degree of idealization which pervades the work as a whole. My new drama is no tragedy in the

ancient sense. What I sought to depict were human beings, and therefore I would not let them talk the 'language of the Gods'.

(*Selected Letters*, pp. 144–5)

The progress towards the play of ideas rather than visions was slow but it was helped by two things: when Ibsen's colleague Bjørnson completed two plays in prose and on contemporary themes which Ibsen recognized as genuinely realistic modern dramas – *A Bankrupt* and *The Editor* – and secondly when his own play *The Pretenders* was acted, in 1876, by the Duke of Meiningen's company.[1] Their production showed Ibsen that the techniques of production and acting were being forged which would be equal to the demands made by his plays. The first play to make such demands was *The Pillars of Society* (1877) which set the style for his future work since it was in prose, on temporary themes and set in Norway. It shows that sharp difference between the speech of individual characters which was to be one of his contributions to modern drama and one of the main difficulties for his translators. In a letter to Rasmus B. Anderson, Professor of Scandinavian Languages at the University of Wisconsin, Ibsen stressed that the dialogue should be kept

as close to ordinary, everyday speech as possible. All turns of speech and inflections that belong only in books must be very carefully avoided in plays, especially in plays like mine, which aim at making the reader or spectator feel that during

[1] This company possibly influenced acting and production techniques as much as Ibsen's plays. The Meiningen Company, formed in 1874, derived its techniques in part from the contemporary English stage and particularly the methods of Charles Kean. Innovations in lighting and scenery (where meticulous attention was paid to accuracy of detail) accompanied one of the first examples of ensemble playing controlled by a director in our modern sense of the word. The Duke excelled in crowd scenes. This company was seen by both Antoine and Stanislavski who thus carried its influences more broadly into the theatre of the twentieth century.

the reading or performance he is actually experiencing a piece
of real life ...

(*Selected Letters*, p. 211)

Very much like *Look Back in Anger* this play opened the eyes
of the young to 'the false tinsel of the theatre that was being
offered us' (quoted Meyer, p. 454) and gave 'the first inkling of a
new world of creative art, when we first felt ourselves face to face
with people of our time, in whom we could believe, and with
a criticism which embraced the whole society of our time' (ibid.,
p. 455). *Ghosts* (1881) was possibly the first great tragedy written
about middle-class people in everyday prose, something we tend
to forget since it now looks to us like a costume drama.

The Duke of Meiningen's troupe had shown Ibsen that a
new style of acting was possible. Life-size characters speaking
ordinary prose required restrained acting rather than a large,
declamatory style; thus neither Bernhardt nor Irving welcomed
Ibsen but Duse did and was to be a great success as Ellida in
The Lady from the Sea. Yet, noticeably, Ibsen was gaining some
curious effects from this ordinary language, distinctive speech
patterns and bourgeois life and was soon to pass from the middle
period of social dramas (*The Pillars of Society* to *An Enemy of
the People*, 1877–82) to those final eight plays which are so much
admired by modern opinion. Ibsen's contemporaries were confused. They found his plays deliberately obscure and sordid.
Certainly the last plays are realistic and concern real people but
we now recognize that they have a symbolism fully integrated
into their prosaic texture. Thus *The Wild Duck* depends on one
symbol, a technique Ibsen used frequently afterwards – and the
characters can never free themselves from this image. Nevertheless Yeats's comment in *The Trembling of the Veil* is quite
characteristic:

I resented being invited to admire dialogue so close to modern
educated speech that music and style were impossible.

(quoted Meyer, p. 632)

Ibsen's views were remarkably consistent; human beings in the social conditions and principles of the day, presented by the actors and scenic designers as true to nature, each character having his own personal way of speaking 'by means of which his degree of education or learning can be noted' (*Selected Letters*, p. 310). Unfortunately this insistence upon naturalness only directed attention to the ideas of the play, and audiences were much struck by what Henry James called 'the positive odour of spiritual paraffin' (*The Scenic Art*, p. 293) without conceding, as James did, that there was more. Indeed realism, which later became naturalism, was becoming less a matter of facing reality and more an anti-romantic insistence upon facing unpleasant realities. Yet Ibsen, for all to see, was using heightened prose – for example the last act of *John Gabriel Borkman* (1896) which his translator Michael Meyer regards as very near to poetry, and even more so in *When We Dead Awaken* (1900) which Meyer feels would have been greater if written in verse. In short Ibsen was a poet who used prose as other poets have used the sonnet form or as Beckett used French: so that confinement can liberate and intensify. Ibsen told Herford (who translated *Brand* into English) that he would probably write his last play once more in verse (quoted Meyer, p. 827): the difficulty was to know which play would be the last.

Ibsen's importance is clear. Naturalism, as any history of drama will show, appears in European theatre wherever we look: Euripides, The Wakefield Shepherds' Plays, *Arden of Faversham* or *The London Merchant*. So Ronald Gaskell expresses the importance of Ibsen perfectly when he writes that his impact in the 1880s was not a change of course 'but an unexpected forward thrust in the same direction' (*Drama and Reality*, London, 1972, p. 61). It is possible that our whole recent venture into modern verse drama so aptly described by George Steiner as exercises in archaeology would not have been necessary if Ibsen and his counterpart Chekhov had written in more accessible places or languages. Or if William Archer and George Bernard Shaw between them had not claimed Ibsen so forcefully as a social dramatist rather than the poetic dramatist he truly was. The English reception of Ibsen stopped short with theme and argument and, as Denis Donoghue remarks, modern theatre-poetry struggles to be born in the shadow of this failure (*The Third Voice*, p. 31). It was this narrow point of view so necessary to Archer and Shaw which obscured the true value of the plays and helped to establish that staple diet of social criticism drama against which verse drama was essentially a protest. Ronald Peacock, in *The Poet in the Theatre*, has noted how few authors tried to maintain the poetic integrity of drama against competition from both outside and inside. Outside there was the novel and the lyric into which in the period since 1870 poetic life has flowed more and more easily, while inside the theatre there was a realistic drama in prose which treated middle-class life and was concerned with social and moral criticism. Thus the social plays of Ibsen, fostered by Shaw, led to a theatre of conflict on a social or moral level in prose and as poets are constantly reminding us prose has its limitations. Even so the history of English drama between 1600 and 1900 does bear out Ibsen's theory that poets should write their plays in prose – an exception being the Irish – and Kenneth Muir, in an essay called 'Verse and Prose', (*Contemporary Theatre*, Stratford-upon-Avon Studies, 4, 1962, pp. 97–115) has suggested that the problem facing the poets was that they imitated literature rather than life, had little immediate relationship with the age in which they wrote and were too little interested in human beings in action. Most of all they never evolved verse which gave the illusion of one man speaking to another, or speaking differently one from another, a situation which he illustrates, cruelly, from *Palicio* by Robert Bridges.

Realism in the hands of Ibsen (and dramatists like Chekhov and Synge) was a reaction against melodrama and the excesses of bad verse, but it replaced these things with a form which gradually lost life through imitation of a superficial kind. And the problem was only partly one of language, of a realism that had reduced 'all stage dialogue to a slangy pattern of one-syllabled words' (T. C. Worsley, *The Fugitive Art*, London, 1952). In his review of Arthur Miller's *Death of a Salesman* (ibid., pp. 93–6) Worsley criticized the play for attempting poetry without words – through symbol, time switches and even lighting, concluding:

> Poetry is made with words; and in the poetic approach, nothing but words will in the last analysis bring success. Mr Kazan may produce as brilliantly as he likes; he may bring out every device of lighting, grouping, stylising, timing and designing to evoke the play's moods. But none of them is an adequate substitute for the words which just aren't there.
>
> (*The Fugitive Art*, p. 96)

T. C. Worsley knows what he is doing, but he is asking for drama as a text, as literature, whereas drama is not entirely literature. Modern drama, as has been increasingly noted, from Ibsen onwards, has relied upon non-verbal symbols, upon images derived from objects that are inanimate and upon a sub-text (what is being said underneath what is being spoken) which carries much of the action that is really only committed to an external reality. In short, the context of Ibsen's plays is the theatre, and however loosely the word 'drama' covers a collection of works of art 'theatre' is the word that even more loosely describes an institution in which a number of talents come together either in harmony or striving for primacy. Theatre recently has been a particularly rich field for experiment and the reader can envisage some of its possibilities from James Roose-Evans's readable account *Experimental Theatre* (London, 1973); even from his opening paragraph:

> For Stanislavski it meant the importance of the actor, whereas for Craig the actor was practically dispensable, the emphasis being upon the scenic possibilities of the theatre. Meyerhold

stressed the importance of the director; Appia the use of light. Brecht, like his master, Piscator, was concerned to explore the didactic nature of the theatre. Artaud, like Stanislavski, came to believe that theatre should reflect not the everyday reality of naturalism but rather those intimations beyond the reach of words.

If we grant that a modern poet could find an appropriate action matched with an appropriate verse form for his play – both natural to our times – that play would still have to compete in the theatre with such other points of view. It is all very well for a poet like Arthur Symons to advance the view:

> The probable words of prose talk can only render a part of what goes on among the obscure imageries of the inner life; for who, in a moment of crisis, responds to circumstances or destiny with an adequate answer? Poetry, which is spoken thought, or the speech of something deeper than thought, may let loose some part of that answer which would justify the soul, if it did not lie dumb upon its lips.

Symons is opposed, with equal conviction, by a director like E. Gordon Craig who writes:

> I am not saying or hinting that the poet is a bad writer of plays or that he has a bad influence upon the theatre, I only wish you to understand that the poet is not of the theatre, has never come from the theatre, and cannot be of the theatre, and that only the dramatist among writers has any birth-claim to the theatre – and that a very slight one.
>
> (*The Theory of the Modern Stage*, edited Eric Bentley, Penguin, 1968, pp. 344–5 and 116)

For Craig even stage directions were useless and impertinent since they usurped the function of the director! When Keats wrote that poetry should be great and unobtrusive, and should startle and amaze not with itself but with its subject he might have had verse dramatists in mind. They claim for language a primacy challenged by actor, director or even the designer of the scenery. And their words are fixed in print, subject to scrutiny; verse nowadays strikes the wrong note of artifice.

As Denis Donoghue points out:

> The 'poetry' of poetic drama is not necessarily or solely a *verbal* construct; it inheres in the structure of the play as a whole. That is, the 'poetry' is not in any one part of the play, or any one of its elements, separately exhibited, but in the manner in which, and the degree to which, all the elements act in cooperation.
>
> (*The Third Voice*, p. 6)

The difficulty of verse has been strikingly stated in Cocteau's famous preface to *Les Mariés de la Tour Eiffel* (1922):

> L'action de ma pièce est imagée tandis que le texte ne l'est pas. J'essaie donc de substituer une 'poésie de théâtre' à la 'poésie au théâtre'. La poésie au théâtre est une dentelle délicate impossible à voir de loin. La poésie de théâtre serait une grosse dentelle; une dentelle en cordages, un navire sur la mer ... Les scènes s'emboîtent comme les mots d'une poème.
> (The action of the play is in images while the text is not: I have tried to substitute a 'poetry of the theatre' for 'poetry in the theatre'. Poetry in the theatre is a piece of lace which it is impossible to see at a distance. Poetry of the theatre would be coarse lace; a lace of ropes, a ship at sea ... The scenes are integrated like the words of a poem.)
>
> (*Théâtre* I, Paris, Gallimard, 15th edition, p. 45)

Cocteau, who classified all his activities under the label of poet and who had early caught the 'red-and-gold disease: theatre-itis' (Francis Steegmuller, *Cocteau*, p. 14) was being anti-literary. He was, of course, much affected by the Diaghilev ballet and, to surprise Diaghilev, produced *Parade* which can lay claim to being the first modern ballet. Apollinaire wrote that this union of painting and dance, of plastic and mime, heralded the advent of a more complete art. It could be objected, however, that all Cocteau's virtuosity did was to produce a stage that was 'handsomely decorated but not as yet lived in' (David Grossvogel, *Twentieth Century French Drama*, New York, 1961, p. 67). But at least there was a recognition that the stage is a space to be filled, and that words have no natural primacy there, a recognition pushed even further by Antonin Artaud. It is easy to see how both were reacting to a garrulous French theatre and overlooked the fact that, to some extent, a stage is a space to be filled by people who act and speak.

Fortunately verse drama in the 1930s and 1940s had actors who were trained to produce the gestures and voice for verbal plays, actors such as Olivier, Gielgud, Richardson, Sybil Thorndike and Edith Evans who played kings and queens as to the manner born and who expected to go one doing so all their life. We should recall at this point that the rapid development of radio and television as well as the cinema has changed the style of acting more thoroughly than the Meininger Troupe could ever hope to do.

The survival, then, of any verse drama at all is remarkable, and any success it achieved would be extraordinary. For the last word must go to prose. Kenneth Tynan reminds us, sensibly, that it has taken a long time to make prose respectable in the theatre and that while no one wishes to banish the luxury of language from the theatre the notion that such luxury is incompatible with prose must go, for prose is 'the most flexible weapon the stage has ever had, and still shining new' ('Notes on a Dead Language', 1955, *Tynan on Theatre*).

2

Poets in the Theatre

In spite of the incompatibility of verse and contemporary dramatic situations, themes and characters, and the fact that verse was no longer at the centre of communication, poets naturally sought to restore their art to its central position in the theatre regardless of prose or producers. The revolt against realism in the theatre was two-fold and the literary attack, in such ways as verse drama, was one, less flamboyant than the anti-literary revolt of Wagner, Cocteau or Artaud. Hostility to the realistic play can be seen in Wagner's combination of music and poetry (though the poetry was strictly subordinated to the music) while Cocteau's brilliant all-round theatre refused to see drama as a literary form but as performance (though it is typical of Cocteau's perversity that when tragedy was dead he decided to revive it and wrote *Renaud et Armide* in 1943 in classical alexandrines); in Artaud's Theatre of Cruelty the emphasis was on spectacle: theatricalities of all kinds, costumes, music, colour, lights, masks, effigies – in short everything but words though these will not be suppressed but merely given the importance they have in dreams (see *The Theatre and Its Double*, 1938).

The more conventional attack by poets on the realistic theatre can easily be overlooked, particularly as it is part of a long history of dreadful mistakes. The restoration of verse tragedy was an obsession with the Romantic poets, and George Steiner's list of their efforts contains William Blake, Wordsworth, Scott, Coleridge, Southey, Landor, Leigh Hunt, Byron, Shelley, Keats and Beddoes. Indeed there are few poets or novelists in the nineteenth century who did not answer the siren call of the theatre: Dickens, Swinburne, Meredith, Stendhal, Balzac, Flaubert, Zola, Dostoevsky, Henry James and Browning (who had the technique, surely, but failed even when writing for Macready) and Tennyson who permitted actors to edit the plays for the stage since he wanted knowledge of the mechanical details!

The failure of the Romantic poets stemmed mainly from a worship of Shakespeare which led them to write their plays by a curious policy of borrowing, illustrated in the following advice from Charles Lamb:

> I recommend a situation like Othello, with relation to Desdemona's intercession for Cassio. By-scenes may likewise receive hints. The son may see his mother at a mask or feast, as Romeo, Juliet ... Dawley may be told his wife's past unchastity at a mask by some witch-character – as Macbeth upon the heath, in dark sentences...
>
> (quoted Steiner, p. 145)

Some Romantic poets saw the danger. Byron thought Shakespeare the worst of models and profited from the recognition and Beddoes, surprisingly, is on record as opposing these vampire-cold reanimations, though it did not prevent him from adding to the haunted ruins of drama.

Matthew Arnold's lament, written in 1879, that we had no drama in England was certainly true though the theatre was undeniably healthy. Thus the delight with which, at the turn of the century, certain verse dramas were received can be explained as a delight in some novelty and a weariness with the realistic manner of Pinero and Jones. In 1900 Beerbohm Tree presented Stephen Phillips's *Herod* at Her Majesty's and critics went berserk, comparing the author with Marlowe, Webster and Chapman. William Archer even compared him with Milton – which may not be complimentary to a dramatist.

It may, of course, have been Tree's spectacular production which succeeded – Phillips said that when he was reading the play to the actor-manager Tree only awoke at the phrase 'trumpets were heard in the distance'. Two years later George Alexander produced *Paolo and Francesca* at the St James's when the poet-dramatist was placed alongside Sophocles and Dante. Phillips had worked for some years as an actor in F. R. Benson's company which at least ensured a sense of theatre in his plays. And audiences clearly yearned to see something other than those meticulous drawing-rooms and hear something other than prose – which perhaps explains the success of J. E. Flecker's *Hassan*, sumptuously mounted at His Majesty's in 1923 with music by Delius. Flecker wisely avoided the use of blank verse but his setting naturally allowed much of the prose to be eastern prose, and lyrical. He died in 1915 having written only one other play, *Don Juan*, which was produced in 1925. In any case his success, as many critics have remarked, may have been due more to what his play had in common with *Chu Chin Chow* than anything else.

Many verse plays performed in the West End are forgotten now, and reading through Allardyce Nicoll's account in *English Drama: 1900–1930*, chapter V, one cannot regret them. Most verse dramatists had no thought of the stage. Their attitudes fostered reading texts and closet dramas on the usual themes: religious, medieval, exotic, classical and renaissance. There are a few surprises. A posthumous printing in 1927 of *Three Plays* by William Archer shows that uncompromising Ibsenite toying with scenes in blank verse, but we have to ask, with Allardyce Nicoll, what prompted someone like John Middleton Murray to waste time and energy writing a blank verse satire on contemporary life called *Cinnamon and Angelica*. Apart from the occasional grim horror[1] the main impression is that writers

---

[1] Interested readers should see Nicoll's account, with illustrations, of W. G. Hole's *Queen Elizabeth* (revised in 1928 from a version of 1904) or Frederic Harrison's Byzantine tragedy *Nicephorus* (1906).

known for poetry, wit and skill seem to become dull and helpless when they turn to the theatre.

Gordon Bottomley argued (and it has been echoed more recently) that audiences needed training for verse but audiences seem to have welcomed the poetic with open arms; it was the sheer bad quality of the plays which consigned them to a decent oblivion. An exception was the Irish theatre, but when John Masefield tried to imitate what the Irish dramatists had done and write a play about the peasants of Gloucestershire and Hereford he produced *The Tragedy of Nan* (1908), generally accepted as one of the most embarrassing plays in the modern theatre.[1] But the Irish theatre is an exception in the modern verse gloom. We are not concerned here with Tynan's view of English drama as an 'Irish conspiracy to make us ashamed of our weakness' but rather with some of the reasons that allowed Irish dramatists to succeed in verse or poetic drama where so many eminent English dramatists failed. There should be an interesting lesson to be learned from the Irish movement in the work of Yeats and Synge. Where English poets had written plays in a way unsuitable for the stage (Tennyson's limited success must be attributed to Irving) there is much in Una Ellis-Fermor's suggestion that the Irish dramatic movement brought back poetry to the English theatre, the poetry that it had missed in Ibsen and if the themes and arguments were not exactly in terms of the society in England they were at least in a language that could be felt without translation. But as she admits, in *The Irish Dramatic Movement* (London, 1939), it is far from easy to pin down the effect particularly as the influence is less definite than that of Ibsen. What advantages, then, did the Irish poet-dramatists have over their English counterparts? Their drama was part of a larger design which hoped to revive a national culture in a country much less affected by the industrial revolution where legendary subjects still seemed to have life in

[1] *The Tragedy of Nan*, however, is highly praised by John Arden as one of the verse plays that influenced him: quot homines, tot sententiae!

them. But where Yeats (by choice) seldom escaped that incubus of verse drama, the coterie theatre, Synge, who used prose, achieved a wider and more assured theatrical success. Both believed in language for Synge thought of Ireland as a place where the imagination of the people 'and the language they use is rich and living', where it was possible for a writer to be 'rich and copious in his words, and at the same time to give the reality, which is the root of all poetry, in a comprehensible and natural form', (*Contemporary Theatre*, Stratford-upon-Avon Studies, 4, 1962, p. 100). But as Kenneth Muir tartly remarks, if peasant speech allowed a kind of prose poetry which was natural a closer look at the dialogue in *The Playboy of the Western World* suggests Rossetti rather than Aran islanders. Nevertheless Synge insisted that it was listening through a chink in the floorboards in an old Wicklow House to maids in the kitchen below which provided him with his material, and that in a good play every speech 'should be as fully flavoured as a nut or apple, and such speeches cannot be written by anyone who works among people who have shut their lips on poetry' (Preface to *The Playboy of the Western World*, written in 1907).

Yeats's choice was deliberate. His industry in forming the Abbey Theatre, helped by the indefatigable Miss Horniman, does not coincide with his idea of the theatre for his own plays. In a letter to Lady Gregory he wrote that he wanted to create 'an unpopular theatre and an audience like a secret society where admission is by favour and never to many ... an audience of fifty, a room worthy of it (some great dining room or drawing room), half-a-dozen young men and women who can dance and speak verse or play drum and flute and zither...' (*The Theory of the Modern Stage*, p. 335), and in *Plays and Controversies* he insisted that actors must move slowly and quietly 'and not very much, and there should be something in their movements decorative and rhythmical as if they were paintings on a frieze' to achieve that leisure 'that is in all fine life – for what we may call the business-will in a high state of activity is not everything, although contemporary drama knows little else' (pp. 132–3). If Yeats is thought of as a poet imposing words on the theatre these views are strangely *theatrical* in their recognition of music and scene albeit in the deliberately chosen aristocratic situation of a man who lived in a grandiose anachronism he naturally called Ireland. Yeats's conscious aim was to 'create for a few people who love symbol a play that will be more a ritual than a play, and leave upon the mind an impression like that of tapestry where the forms only half-reveal themselves amid the shadowy folds' (programme note quoted *The Third Voice*, pp. 33–4).

Yeats was willing to mix prose and verse in the same play and often wrote Jacobean blank verse. *The Shadowy Waters* was written in verse in 1900 and then rewritten to increase tension by juxtaposing prose and verse. As with Arden the prose mirrors the human world while the Higher Reality expresses itself in verse. Peter Ure has traced the history of *The Countess Cathleen* (1899) which enjoyed, if that be the word, five major revisions over thirty years and finally appeared as a stage version and a reading version! (See *Yeats the Playwright*, London, 1963, chapter 1.)

Yeats was aware of the problems; in *Poems 1899–1905* he wrote:

It is not very difficult to construct a fairly vigorous prose play, and then ... decorate it and encumber it with poetry. But a play of that kind will never move us poetically, because it does not uncover, as it were, that high, intellectual, delicately organized soul of man and of an action, that may not speak aloud if it do not speak in verse.

(pp. xi–xii)

Yeats thought the mixture of verse and prose could be useful in four ways summed up by Donoghue in *The Third Voice* (pp. 40–1): prose could correct rhetorical excesses and help the audience; prose could be used when a play has a double plot, especially if the secondary plot is in any way a burlesque of the main plot; the juxtaposition of prose and verse could show the actual and the ideal, our partial (realistic) view as opposed to the full view; and, finally, verse was useful for a chorus which could provide a ritual contrast with the naturalistic prose sections.

The model at hand was the Japanese Noh play being translated by Ezra Pound and, possibly, by Yeats himself. Both Arthur Waley and Fenellosa had insisted that these plays were analogous to Greek and Elizabethan theatre in their religious origins and could be used as models to restore drama to its original power, evoking a sacred presence with all the devices of ceremony, dance, poetry and scenery – a ritual that comes close to fulfilling the demands of Artaud. The aims and repertoire of Noh were firmly established by the middle of the fifteenth century and the isolation of Japan and the patronage of the richest and most powerful families ensured its survival as an art form. The words may not be very important (the texts date from the time of Chaucer and are, anyway, muffled by the masks) but the finest poetry is used in combination with music, masks and dancing. The avoidance of realism is complete, everything inessential is excluded and the subjects are those basic emotions – love, hate and jealousy – which inspire most drama. The technical demands upon both performers and audience ensure that it is a minority theatre but it did offer Yeats a theatre form of historical importance which did more than merely represent life. It was, however, a curious form for a dramatist to choose who is often described as sacrificing everything to verse.

His finest verse drama is probably *Purgatory* written in 1938 and produced at the Abbey in the same year, when Eliot noted, with satisfaction, that Yeats had moved away from the blank verse in which he had trusted for many years. The scene of the play is now strikingly familiar: a ruined house with a bare tree in the background. Outside the ruin, in the moonlight, stand a pedlar and his bastard son. This was the house where the pedlar was born, offspring of the great lady who married her drunken groom and died in childbirth. The pedlar grew up resentful of the wealth squandered by his father and on his sixteenth birthday, when his father accidentally set fire to the house, stabbed his father dead and fled.

This is the anniversary of that wedding night when the spirit of the lady must re-enact the arrival of her groom and the sexual act that begot the pedlar. Hoofbeats are heard and the pedlar can see the bride in lighted windows. His son mocks him and tries to steal the bag of money the pedlar carries, threatening to kill him. But while this is happening the spirit of the groom leans out of the window and the son sees him and cowers away as the pedlar stabs him to death. The windows darken, the phantom has been exorcised but as the old pedlar bends down to pick up the scattered coins he hears hoofbeats again and realizes that though he has ended the pollution – his bastard will not get another bastard – the vigil of the dead lady goes on:

> Twice a murderer and all for nothing,
> And she must reanimate that dead night
> Not once but many times!

The play ends with the prayer that God will release the soul from its torment; man can do no more.

Purgatory, however splendid, is a *very* short play. It offers no clues to the solution of full-scale drama in verse. Nevertheless there is a recognition of theatrical needs. The choice of an aristocratic drama was deliberate – and Yeats's plays, whether in verse or prose, draw their power from myth and symbol. And like Eliot Yeats does realize that the verse is only part of a dramatic communication. Though neither had much affinity with theatre in its fullest commercial sense they saw the social nature of that theatre, turning to it rather in the service of their art than from any natural inclination.

It was the social nature of the theatre which attracted poets like Auden and Isherwood who used it to serve their ends rather than because they liked the theatre. Auden and Isherwood used verse to evoke some special response without calling attention to the verse itself. It was a rhetorical aid to jerk an audience into listening while at the same time it hinted that the plot had deeper implications. The plot itself proceeds in prose. As early as 1926 Auden was criticizing theatre and stating that

> the only remaining traces of theatrical art were to be found on the music hall stage: the whole of modern realistic drama since Tchekhov had got to go; later, perhaps, something might be done with puppets.
>
> (*Lions and Shadows*, p. 215)

Paid on Both Sides (1928) – a charade – is nearly closet drama but in 1932 Auden, with Rupert Doone and Robert Medley, founded the Group Theatre which gave him an opportunity for writing plays that could be staged. Often linked with Brecht Auden, in fact, remains strictly faithful to native forms like the music hall and pantomime: witness his programme note to *The Dance of Death*:

> Drama is essentially the art of the body. The basis of acting is acrobatics, dancing and all forms of physical skill. The music hall, the Christmas pantomime, and the country house charade are the most living dramas of today.
>
> (quoted John Fuller, *A Reader's Guide to W. H. Auden*, London, 1970, p. 77)

But theatre was always a sideline for the poet. *The Dance of Death* (1930) was written for and danced by Rupert Doone but since Auden disliked ballet this experiment was never repeated and it has been out of print since 1953. It was intended to popularize Marx and John Fuller defends the choruses by saying that they were deliberately written as doggerel. Much more successful was *The Dog Beneath the Skin* (1936) which deserves revival, and in which Isherwood thought of himself as the librettist to Auden as composer. This fable of the search for a missing heir by a young man with a dog who travels through revolution, the red light district, to fall from grace in the Nineveh Hotel, from which he is rescued by the missing heir (who has been beneath the dog skin all the time) has its amusing moments and its serious points – particularly when they return to find sinister changes have taken place in the village. But the vaudeville treatment of cultural ills seriously undermines the satire, turning evils into peccadilloes so that we laugh at their absurdity and the social message often seems to be there to make the comedy go round. The pair are now mainly remembered for *The Ascent of F6*, produced in 1937 by Rupert Doone with music by Benjamin Britten. Isherwood did the plot here which is more involved and the play is called a tragedy and concerns the motives of Ransom whose story seems to be based on T. E. Lawrence in the predicament of Captain Scott (or Mallory) with the emotional problems of Hamlet.

The play opens with Ransom reading Dante (on Virtue and Knowledge) in Wastdale where he is staying with Gunn, Shaw-cross, Lamp and Dr Williams until his brother Sir James arrives from the Colonial Office to ask him to scale the Haunted Mountain, F6 and win both Sudolands for Britain (and her investments there). Ransom refuses the blandishments of patriotism and money until his mother arrives to explain her relationship, in verse, with her two sons, when Ransom agrees. Auden intersperses these scenes in prose and verse with comment from the stage boxes. In the right box the A family to whom nothing happens:

MR A Has anything happened?

MRS A   What should happen?
  The cat has died at Ivy Dene,
  The Crowthers' pimply son has passed Matric,
  St. Neots has put up light blue curtains,
  Frankie is walking out with Winnie

And Georgie loves himself. What should happen?
Nothing that matters will ever happen.
MR A No, nothing that matters will ever happen;
Nothing you'd want to put in a book;
Nothing to tell to impress your friends –
The old old story that never ends:
The eight o'clock train, the customary place,
Holding the paper in front of your face,
The public stairs, the glass swing-door,
The peg for your hat, the linoleum floor,
The office stool and the office jokes
And the fear in your ribs that slyly pokes:
Are they satisfied with you?

(*Ascent*, p. 18)

In Act II there is a prose discussion between Ransom and
the Abbot on the Demon of the Mountain, with some character analysis (in prose) and echoes of the temptation scene from
Murder in the Cathedral, while the As are delighted with the
expedition which they see as the salvation of England:

MR A England's honour is covered with rust.
MRS A Ransom must beat them! He must! He must!
MR A Or England falls. She has had her hour
And now must decline to be a second-class power.

(*Ascent*, p. 82)

Unfortunately the climb is as good as its climbers and Lamp
is killed by an avalanche in pursuit of a rare plant, Shawcross
walks off the edge of a cliff because Ransom chooses Gunn for
the ascent, Gunn dies on the way to the top and Ransom
struggles on. Back in the stage boxes even the Radio Announcer
(Stage Box left) goes into verse on the boredom of no news
until finally the two boxes come together in a duet, 'like people
speaking in their sleep':

LEFT BOX	RIGHT BOX
No news	
	Useless to wait
Too late	
	Their fate
	We do not know
Snow on the pass	
	Alas
Nothing to report	
	Caught in the blizzard
Fought through the storm	
	Warm in our beds we wonder
Thunder and hail	
	Will they fail? Will they miss their success
Yes. They will die	
	We sigh. We cannot aid
They fade from our mind	
	They find no breath
But Death	

(*Ascent*, p. 107)

And Death takes the form of a veiled figure on the summit who, after a chorus of monks, hovers over an argument between Ransom and his brother, and who turns out to be Mother claiming her son at last. The stage is left empty except for the body of Ransom on the summit of F6.

Whether we believe with Justin Repogle (*Auden's Poetry*, London, 1969) that collecting is a 'familiar neurotic practice of anal-retentive types, a socially respectable channel for their special perverse pleasure' collecting, for Auden, is certainly an occupation of the enemy and both Gunn and Lamp point up the general sickness of this mountain team which strikes an outsider as an odd collection of cripples to send up a mountain. Personally I join those critics who feel that the play's message emerges, if at all, fuzzily rather than those who point to its skill in appealing on so many levels (adventure story, boredom of suburban life which demands heroes, and scrutiny of hero's mother fixation or spiritual pride). What is clear, as F. R. Leavis pointed out in 'Mr. Auden's Talent' (*Scrutiny*, vol. V, 3 December 1936, p. 325), is that the play is heavily parasitic on the Eliot of *Sweeney* and the Choruses. This play and its successor, *On The Frontier* (1938), appealed to a minority audience and it could be said that in the cause of the topical (which is not negligible in the theatre) Auden sacrificed dramatic integrity. The same might be said of Stephen Spender's *Trial of a Judge* (1938) – a tragic statement in five acts – written for Rupert Doone and the Group Theatre. This is a play about the problems of Law, Justice and Politics starting with the murder of a communist Polish Jew. The verse does nothing beyond produce a kind of elevated atmosphere for an argument that is powerful and will always be relevant but there is no attempt at characterization and the villains, who are stereotypes, are given weak verse.

American poets who came into the theatre such as E. E. Cummings, William Carlos Williams, Robert Lowell, Wallace Stevens, Eberhart and MacLeish are all poets who come into a coterie theatre to make a second reputation and the limitations of coterie theatre, particularly its short life, are clear. Such poets tend to be verbally indulgent (and why not if the play has little chance of being staged) writing dramatic poems rather than drama. Here, too, in the area of the topical or the satirical the problem of domestic naturalism occurs. Realism is lost if characters speak in verse and if they speak in prose that sense of some higher reality or universal quality which transcends the merely topical goes. We need look no further than Archibald Mac-Leish's *Panic* (1936) where bankers faced by the Great Crash chant, partly as a chorus and partly reciting modern and impressionistic poetry, neither of which, as Bamber Gascoigne remarks, are activities particularly close to the reality of a modern banker's existence (*Twentieth Century Drama*, London, 1962). Metre seems to inhibit vital characters in our time.

One obvious escape is into a remote domestic situation where verse strikes a less discordant note: historical drama. It is unkind to pin this label on Maxwell Anderson since his intention was serious and nothing less than bringing back blank verse to the theatre. Anderson dominated the theatre in America during the 1930s as O'Neill did that of the 1920s. Yet he was an alien voice since he persisted in writing poetic and romantic tragedies.[1] Anderson had thought about tragedy and verse and in his essay 'A Prelude to Poetry in the Theater' defends verse as the language of emotion while prose is the language of information. Those plays which make a journalistic comment on our social, economic and political life are all very well but there are mysteries – a sentiment which other poetic dramatists have echoed, including Fry.

Elizabeth the Queen (1930) has, obviously, heroic characters and a tragic situation (Essex and his fatal flaw) but the play turns out to be a sentimental tragedy while Elizabeth and Essex remain, in spite of what they do, rather too nice to be alive. Anderson mingles verse and prose – thus the council scene in Act III is in prose which shifts into verse when Elizabeth and Essex face one another alone. *Winterset* (1935) moved the action into contemporary life and meets the usual difficulties since it requires gangsters and a judge to talk in iambic pentameters; and *Key Largo* was another attempt to treat contemporary events as verse tragedy.

Apart from costume drama and coterie theatre one of the great possibilities for verse drama was radio broadcasting. The success, for example, of Louis MacNeice's *The Dark Tower* suggested, though MacNeice is another Irishman, that is medium was a perfect home with a considerable audience since it neatly sidesteps the problems of an acted, visible performance

[1] See Vincent Wall, 'Maxwell Anderson, The Last Anarchist', *American Drama and Its Critics*, edited A. S. Downer, Chicago, 1965, pp. 147–76.

and throws everything on to sound, and particularly the words. This success seemed consolidated by Dylan Thomas's *Under Milk Wood*, a play in prose albeit Welsh-prose. But the serious purpose of the play – a comment on the world gone mad by a village which had been declared mad – was soon lost and the 'poetry' essentially decorates what has become a comic action; and it is the comedy that we admire. Moreover the radio yielded too swiftly to television (in which the old battle between words and scenery is renewed) with economic implications for the writer. All of which tended to diminish an ideal outlet for verse drama.

So far we have considered the British experience of poets in the theatre mainly because the response of verse rests upon an intimacy with language and foreign languages do not easily yield up their secrets in verse. The English-language experience is not uncharacteristic. In the French theatre a crucial date would be 1928 when Giraudoux produced *Siegfried*, replacing the well-made play with a well-written play. For Giraudoux poetry, as with Anderson, was the only force that could tame tragedy and make it bearable to an audience and his rhetoric certainly restored the word which Cocteau had banished, though clearly Giraudoux had taken a close look at Cocteau's theatricalism and learned its advantages. French dramatists have always been long-winded and theatricalism under Cocteau and Artaud flourished in rebellion against words, but Giraudoux restored the monologue and tirade to a world where even valets speak verse. But for Giraudoux it was: Thalia before and Jouvet afterwards – so his theatre of language is always a theatre of acted language. Jouvet was a student of Copeau and therefore respectful of the text and like Copeau he believed that sets should look like sets, that the action should be simple but self-consciously so and the text spoken slowly, and he used all the pomp of spectacle to make the text live. Giraudoux himself declared that language had a phonetic and affective value and like Claudel did not bother to accommodate style to character.

Claudel, who aimed in his plays to combine the speech of theatre and the poetry of language (and his admirers claim that he succeeded) had the help of Jean-Louis Barrault, and composed speech sounds as if they were musical notes, basing his verse on the rhythm of breathing – but again character tends to be shadowy, and the monologues hold up rather than assist the action's forward movement. Claudel, too, was enthusiastic for Noh plays as an escape from what Dullin called the 'frightful natural'.

Other poets writing for the stage included Apollinaire, Audiberti, Supervielle, Schehadé and Pichette (who wrote one play completely in alexandrines) and these followed the two regular verse dramatists of the French stage: Francois Porché and Maurice Rostand. Critics generally agree that the movement for verse drama more or less ceases after the First World War because, paradoxically, a feeling for poetry was strong in the rising generations of audiences and they found verse dull and uninspired: Giraudoux's poetic prose was more vital than all the couplets of Rostand. In short Giraudoux and Claudel were aiming at poetic rather than verse drama. And the same could be said of Lorca writing in Spain.

Lorca has written poetry that lives naturally upon the stage but his career shows the elimination of verse. After *Mariana Pineda* (1927), his first major play, Lorca writes substantially in prose reserving verse for moments of exceptional intensity. There is no sign that Lorca sought an all-purpose rhythm in which conversation could be carried out. When verse is used it is exceptional, formal and taut, usually an eight-syllable line with repetition and assonance to tighten the lines and close every second line. Thus though he sacrifices that unity which a single line might have produced he gains in dramatic contrast. His prose works as poetry at the right moments as *The House of Bernarda Alba* (1936), which contains no verse, shows. He was murdered after this play so we shall never know how great a poet of the theatre he might have become. And, of course, his

Spanish setting, like an Irish setting, is to an English audience remote, strange and romantic or foreign enough to permit the language to seem natural; and, as with Chekhov and Ibsen, translation is a considerable source of confusion.

3

Religious Verse Drama

In their appeal to the music hall, charade, pantomime and circus the verse dramatists were taking hold of rituals which were less and less part of everyday life, and they were using verse which even in poetry was less and less a dominant medium. There was one institution, also fading, which was an obvious home for verse drama and non-realistic presentation since it lived in two worlds and dealt naturally with the interaction of those worlds by ritual, emblematic colours and elevated language. But the Church faced the problem of being shown to be relevant to contemporary life though the problem was less acute for a dramatist since his audience, a congregation, was not merely accustomed to language and ritual but also was accustomed to being bored or puzzled in the interest of moral uplift or spiritual consolation. The relationship between religion and art is confusing, and verse adds to the confusion, but of course religious verse drama is a coterie theatre and basically irrelevant to the problem of verse in the theatre of our time.

Ronald Duncan's *This Way To The Tomb!* (1945) was a commercial success but a rare one among poets like Norman Nicholson and Anne Ridler who wrote verse dramas, but as lyric poets, and the lyric art strangles drama. Charles Williams is the most notable dramatist in this protected context. He wrote more than nine plays which are as much a part of his religious view of life as his poetry, criticism, theological writings and novels. His most famous play is *Thomas Cranmer of Canterbury* (1936), performed the year after *Murder in the Cathedral* at

Canterbury. Williams is formal at all times which is consonant
with his sense of ceremony as the expression of divine order.
Judgement at Chelmsford (1939) was not performed until after
his death and his last play *Terror of Light* is in prose but he
intended to rewrite it in verse.

Thomas Cranmer of Canterbury is a Brecht-like sequence of
incidents in the life of Cranmer, that quiet, studious man
elevated by Henry, responsible for the English Bible and the
Book of Common Prayer and ultimately martyred under Mary.
The character, or figure of the Skeleton who argues, comments on and creates the action, is a good invention and
helps us portray the spiritual conflict and there is a choral
use of priests or Lords which is natural in the context of the
Church:

THE FIRST LORD	Most mighty sir, regard the spirituality.
THE SECOND LORD	Regard, most mighty sir, the sins of the monks.
THE FIRST LORD	Reckon meadow and pasture – one-fourth the realm.
THE SECOND LORD	Compute paten and pyx, chalice and cope.
THE FIRST LORD	Sir, the need of the government!
THE SECOND LORD	The simplicity of Christ!
THE FIRST LORD	Sir, for the Crown's need's sake –
THE SECOND LORD	for Christ's gospel's sake –
BOTH THE LORDS	it were right the Lord of England received the richness.
THE FIRST LORD	Inflaming their bestial appetite with spiri-tual lust,
THE SECOND LORD	fornications with pomp, adulteries with power,
THE FIRST LORD	betraying the poor vows they swore to keep,
THE SECOND LORD	abusing their virginal conformity with Christ's mind,

THE FIRST LORD	basely and turbulently collecting earth's treasure,
THE SECOND LORD	besides fornications and adulteries of the common sort,
THE FIRST LORD	such as we dare not name for mere modesty,
THE SECOND LORD	whereby their heart's brothers enrich damnation,
BOTH THE LORDS	it were well the Lords of England had their wealth.

(Collected Plays, p. 15)

This works very well indeed with sufficient character, motive and irony but not too much.

Judgement at Chelmsford was more strictly a pageant, an exhibition (according to the author's prologue) of the Church's ways of living and how far and with what energy she had followed God. It consists of eight episodes (e.g. The Chelmsford Witches, The Reformation, Old King Cole, St Helena and the Invention of the Cross) with a prologue and epilogue. The scene of Modern Life with Machine Workers on one side and Agricultural Labourers on the other battling for a young couple with characters like A Critical Lady, A Firm Man and The Well-Meaning Lady has something to say but scarcely says it in an unstilted manner. Verse and prose are mixed in this pageant.

Seed of Adam (1937), a nativity play which sees the overthrow of the destructive cannibal nature of man (an image that recurs in *The House of the Octopus* and which, as Katharine Worth has remarked, connects Williams with, of all people, Edward Bond) was followed by two more Christmas plays, *The Death of Good Fortune* and *The House by the Stable* where Pride and Hell dice with Man for his soul when the servant Gabriel asks Man to assist a young man and his pregnant wife. Pride objects to having them in the house and so they are allowed to use the stable. Williams wrote a sequel called *Grab and Grace* in which Pride and Hell, somewhat bedraggled, return to find Man living with Faith and Grace.

In *The House of the Octopus*, written for the United Council for Missionary Education, the story of a tropical island invaded to destroy Christianity had overtones of topicality which were never intended. The author, in a note, apologised for the sophisticated verse that the natives speak and a metaphysical cast of thought hardly appropriate to South Sea Islanders, putting his finger on a great problem of modern verse drama:

> the effort after simplicity in verse is likely to end in mere silliness; outside lyric, its achievement is on the whole the mark of the greatest poets in their greatest moments.

Williams's own language hovers between the pompous and the colloquial or what passes for colloquial in verse drama. It is the failure to produce verse which expresses character and individuality as much as it captures the modern tone which is so fatal.

Religious drama in verse is restricted in every sense but it was part of that larger yearning to escape the merely social, moral and physical. The poets began to reconsider the possibilities of both language and the theatre; they provided roles in plays which trained actors and audiences, teaching the latter to listen, and listen seriously. Something was needed to revitalize the British stage and after *Murder in the Cathedral* that something could well have been verse drama. It is easily forgotten how trivial, how merely entertaining, most of what occupied the stage was. R. C. Sherriff, in *No Leading Lady*, recalls:

> People went to the theatre for clever acting, an intriguing variety of scenes, fascinating actresses in eye-catching clothes; they expected fine speeches, witty dialogue, a story to excite them with unexpected twists and turns.

The 1920s had been mainly a period of slight plays by forgotten writers, and actresses like Marie Tempest, Yvonne Arnaud and Gertrude Lawrence devoted their careers almost entirely to comedy, as did du Maurier, Coward or Charles Hawtrey. There was very little Shakespeare – though John Barrymore's *Hamlet* in 1925 was obviously successful – and it was one of the theatrical revolutions that the heroic actors who spoke the verse drama of the 1930s and 1940s so elegantly were thought to be intellectually rigorous when compared with the generation that preceded them, just as they were to appear superficial and artificial to a generation that followed with Brecht, the Absurd and the Kitchen Sink. But their good voices and strong, physical presence enabled them to do remarkable things with the classics like Shakespeare and Chekhov. It was natural in the context of the theatre as well as that of serious drama that verse dramatists should aim at creating heroic characters.

Dramatists as diverse as Eliot, Cocteau, Yeats and Lorca have one thing in common: hostility to the nineteenth-century realistic play. They sought, to borrow the words of Francis Fergusson, to make their audiences 'transcend the narrow shrewdness of the modern city, and to comprehend human life in the wider perspectives of ancient sources'. Thus, they brought back a wider sense of theatre, either by reviving the classics or, indirectly, by using myth, folk traditions, the circus, the charade – theatre forms of some antiquity and outside the scope of modern realism. They restored ceremony – either with words as in verse drama or without them as in the theatre of Cocteau and Artaud. The groundwork they did in shaking up theatre, in suggesting that it was a place where serious matters happened and could be discussed, is more important than their relative merits. And no one is more crucial in this than the religious verse dramatist T. S. Eliot.

4

T. S. Eliot

The career of T. S. Eliot in the theatre has been well docu-
mented and nowhere better than in E. Martin Browne, *The
Making of T. S. Eliot's Plays* (London, 1969) and D. E. Jones,
The Plays of T. S. Eliot (London, 1960), to both of which all
subsequent writers, including myself, owe a great debt. If it
were not for Eliot's 'success' in the commercial theatre it would
not be necessary to treat the subject of verse drama in our
modern period seriously. Here, however, is a great poet and
critic whose mature work is in drama and who has confessed
that he has had before him for many years 'the mirage of the
perfection of verse drama' (*On Poetry and Poets*, p. 87) and if
the image of a mirage is unfortunately suggestive Mr Eliot nevertheless had 'an incentive towards further experiment and
exploration, beyond any goal which there is prospect of attaining'
(ibid., p. 86). Denis Donoghue, in *The Third Voice*, devotes
chapters 5 to 10 (out of sixteen) to the plays of T. S. Eliot but
it is difficult to judge how far his praise is consciously ambiva-
lent. *Murder in the Cathedral* is an act of piety before it is a
work of art (p. 92), *The Family Reunion* shows Eliot yielding
to the temptation of being poetical, indulging in purely verbal
activity at the expense of dramatic relevance and propriety
(p. 98) and even *The Confidential Clerk*, which Donoghue
admires, shows how Eliot 'ingratiates' himself with the audience
by introducing them to two worlds they know or can imagine,
Art and Commerce, arousing no doctrinal suspicions. *The Elder
Statesman*, we are told, works like all his plays, 'tricking' audi-

ences into analogues of worship (p. 158). Such comments raise questions. They certainly suggest the social purpose of the plays for it is almost as if Eliot were following Ibsen's dictum that people went to the theatre to be amused but their eyes could be opened as well from the stage as from a pulpit, 'especially as so many people no longer go to church' (quoted Meyer, p. 659). But the problem with Eliot is not simply a distinction between theory and practice, it is rather the failure of nerve on the poet's part paralleled only by the example of Henry James who was also willing to jettison anything for the unholy trade of the theatre.

Nevertheless the work of T. S. Eliot represents the most complete attempt to construct a theory of drama since Dryden, at the end of a career which established him as a most persuasive authority. The theatre is obviously a set of conventions, one of which is language. The Elizabethans mixed genres as easily as they mixed verse and prose; confidently but not from any policy. Naturalism excludes verse as the language of a play because its organization is too obvious and offends the natural-ness of the action. So the first objection to prose is this very naturalness, which limits, tending to emphasize 'the ephemeral and superficial; if we want to get at the permanent and universal we tend to express ourselves in verse' (*Selected Essays*, p. 46). Most advocates of verse drama suggest this in one form or another though Tynan's objection remains: prose is a new instru-ment and its possibilities seem inexhaustible. Moreover, as Steiner points out, when Eliot grants that Ibsen and Chekhov achieved effects which he thought only poetry could achieve the concession is grudging – they seem to have been 'hampered in expression by writing in prose' (*On Poetry and Poets*, pp. 86–7).

Secondly verse must be organic, not decoration; a medium to look through not at – as Eliot expressed it in a letter to Pound (quoted D. E. Jones, p. 11). If poetry (Eliot means verse) is organic then Eliot believed he could achieve a kind of double-ness of action, not to be confused with allegory or symbolism.

This was to be a sort of under-pattern to which all things must be subordinated even if this means a loss of character. Thus characters are not depicted with psychological realism but as types with just enough characteristics to be individuals as well. This loss, which is serious in the theatre, would be compensated for by gaining several planes of reality – which again may not be a theatrical compensation.

The greatest problem facing any verse dramatist (as the Romantic poets dramatically illustrate) was Shakespeare. A pale imitation of Elizabethan blank verse could only be artificial in the worst sense, and could be no contribution to the drama of our time ('The Need for Poetic Drama', *The Listener*, 25 November 1936). Verse drama now must not merely overcome the fact that verse is no longer at 'the centre of communicative discourse' (Steiner, p. 309) and avoid being a grave-robber, it must also relate to common speech striking an audience as being how they would talk if they could talk poetry (*On Poetry and Poets*, p. 31). Thus Eliot believed that previous failures had had nothing to do with plot or character but with the speech given to characters which had been 'something that we cannot associate with any human being except a poetry reciter' (ibid., p. 34).

He seemed the poet with the right qualities to solve this problem. One of his main achievements had been to bring back into poetry prosaic words, including those from routine middle-class life. His poetry had been contemporary, had portrayed the inter-action of past on present (using myth as well as allusions to poems of other times), had been dramatic (his personae can be heard whispering through *The Waste Land*): he had, in short, combined the richly colloquial and the obviously poetic. His desire to write plays about contemporary life dates back as early as 1924, if Arnold Bennett's comment that Eliot wanted to write a drama of modern life, 'furnished flat sort of people', is accurate (see D. E. Jones, p. 27). In many ways his first attempt *Sweeney* (1926–7) with its echoes of the music hall, its modern tone and satirical bite was very successful, but the play is in fragments and, as Ronald Gaskell points out, when a play runs for two or three hours 'the pressure of everyday life in a drawing-room set becomes inexorable. The verse line relaxes into elegant conversation; metaphor, the most precise and dramatic kind of speech, goes out of the window.' (*Drama and Reality*, London, 1972). Eliot observed that an Elizabethan audience wanted entertainment of a crude sort but 'would *stand* a great deal of poetry' (*The Sacred Wood*, p. 70), and so his first audience was one that would stand a great deal of poetry. For Eliot moved into the theatre deliberately. He perceived that it was not only artistic conventions that were lacking but also social and moral conventions; his progress as a persuader is from the Church to little theatre to Festival plays to commercial theatre – a gradual movement towards a play about modern life in verse.

George Bell became Bishop of Chichester in 1929, appointing E. Martin Browne as Director of Religious Drama for the diocese in 1930 and that same year Eliot visited the Palace at Chichester. But it was not until 1934 that the poet became directly involved with the stage by providing verse for a scenario in aid of the Forty-Five Churches Fund, a pageant which aimed to show the work of the churches in the present day. The show was modelled on a revue where chorus girls kept the audience's attention by their charms. Here a chorus of voices (the physical charms were hidden in stiff hessian costumes and half-masks designed by Stella Pearce) was intended to do the same. This was Eliot's second voice (poet addressing audience) rather than the third voice where the poet attempts to create a dramatic character. The use of chorus had precedents. Gilbert Murray's translations of Greek tragedy had been published in 1905 and the chorus was trained by Elsie Fogerty who had been working on the art of choral speaking since 1900. Gordon Bottomley had used a chorus in 1933 for *The Acts of Saint Peter* performed in Exeter Cathedral. *The Rock* was produced at Sadler's Wells in 1934 and though Eliot used the Greek chorus he took his versification from *Everyman*. The choruses clearly allowed for verse and expressed the community voice but Eliot rejected the idea that he was simply copying Greek drama, pointing out that many of their conventions were now inappropriate – the chorus holds up the action and talks too much. He agreed that some uses were, however, still available:

> It mediates between action and the audience; it intensifies the action by projecting its emotional consequences, so that we as the audience see it doubly, by seeing its effect on other people.
>
> ('The Need for Poetic Drama', *The Listener*,
> 25 November 1936)

George Bell was in the audience and asked Eliot to write a play for the Canterbury Festival of 1935.[1] Thus Eliot began his dramatic career properly as in Greek tragedy by showing the story of a cult at the sacred spot associated with that cult. He was also discussing another project of a more secular kind with Ashley Dukes and Rupert Doone. Dukes had put the money from a recent successful comedy into buying an old Sunday School in Notting Hill Gate where his wife (Marie Rambert) was to work with her ballet company in a small theatre, The Mercury. This theatre was used by E. Martin Browne under the auspices of CEMA for several seasons of verse drama from 1945 to 1948 with some assistance from the Arts Council. Browne believed strongly that poetry and drama had been divorced too long and that the stage needed verse to lift its diction above the commonplace. The Poet's Theatre Guild was established in 1946 producing plays by T. S. Eliot, Fry, Humbert Woolf and Gordon Bottomley. Rupert Doone who had staged *Sweeney Agonistes* in 1934 had been a dancer with Diaghilev until the impresario died in 1929 and it was he who urged Eliot

[1] Bell had started this Festival in 1928 with Masefield's *The Coming of Christ*, the proceeds from which had gone into a fund to commission plays. Eliot was the first to be asked, followed by Charles Williams, Dorothy Sayers, Christopher Hassall and Christopher Fry *inter alia*. Tennyson's *Becket* was performed in 1932 and 1933 and Laurence Binyon's *The Young King* was ready for 1934.

to use more verse and suggested the device of the Four Tempters in *Murder in the Cathedral* (E. Martin Browne, pp. 39, 43).

In *Murder in the Cathedral* Eliot based his verse line again on *Everyman* and his structure on Greek tragedy, but in 1936, curiously, he believed that it was necessary to emphasize that the play was written in verse. The Chorus was an advance on *The Rock*, being no longer anonymous but having what Elsie Fogerty called 'threads of character' in their speaking:

> Seven years and the summer is over
> Seven years since the Archbishop left us,
> He who was always kind to his people.
> But it would not be well if he should return.
> King rules or barons rule;
> We have suffered various oppression,
> But mostly we are left to our own devices,
> And we are content if we are left alone.
> We try to keep our households in order;
> The merchant, shy and cautious, tries to compile a little
> > fortune,
> And the labourer bends to his piece of earth, earth colour,
> > his own colour,
> Preferring to pass unobserved.
> Now I fear the disturbance of the quiet seasons:
> Winter shall come bringing death from the sea,
> Ruinous spring shall beat at our doors,
> Root and shoot shall eat our eyes and our ears,
> Disastrous summer burn up the beds of our streams
> And the poor shall wait for another decaying October...
>
> > (*Murder in the Cathedral*, p. 12)

The structure of the play as it builds up the story of Thomas through Chorus, priests, Tempters and Thomas himself leads to a prose interlude followed by the arrival of the Knights and their self-justification (in prose). *Murder in the Cathedral*, like

Hoffmansthal's *Jedermann* (1890), occurred in a non-theatrical setting but did attract a wide cross-section of society. However that audience remained a congregation and in this sense although the play compels admiration (and it does) it offers no solution to the problem of modern verse drama. It has, moreover, a historical subject, a ritual setting and it was presented to ears familiar with liturgical language and willingly there to witness the subject of martyrdom. The play is at its worst when it moves into prose and the problems of the 1930s in the speeches of the Knights and it was to this modernity that Eliot had to turn. He had produced not a drama of modern life but something in the Georgian tradition of verse drama: remote subject, exalted language and minority audience. His idea of the social usefulness of verse was being fulfilled only in a limited way since he wished to convey the pleasures of poetry 'not only to a larger audience, but to larger groups of people collectively; and the theatre is the best place in which to do it' (*The Use of Poetry and The Use of Criticism*, p. 154).

When he moved into commercial theatre Eliot recognized that he could no longer move between verse and prose since in that context verse would be unnatural and the shock would be not to make people aware of a deeper purpose but that the language was odd. Audiences would be listening to verse as verse rather than to what it was doing. Eliot believed that he faced two problems, one at least of which was real, in writing a play in verse about the Christian life. He had to fight an ignorance of Christian principles and a prejudice against them, and he had to rehabilitate verse. Audience response to Fry suggests that Eliot was over-cautious in his second task. He rejected blank verse and looked back to the root principle of English prosody: stress rather than number. He devised a line of varying lengths with a fixed number of stresses (normally three) and a caesura coming after the first or second stress, and he hoped this line would be capable of all kinds of conversation from the drawing-room at teatime to 'the revelations of the heart's depth and the terror of eternal things' (E. Martin Browne, quoted D. E. Jones, p. 85). Using this multi-purpose line Eliot sought a double action based on myth. But unlike the French dramatists he did not start with the myth and allow the audience to make the connection, he started with ordinary characters who gradually appear to be in the same plight as their Greek models. Both solutions were disastrous and particularly that used by Eliot. Hugh Dickinson, examining the use of myth by ten modern dramatists in *Myth on the Modern Stage* (University of Illinois, 1969) complains that Eliot uses myth so completely as a private guide to order his own creations that the myths are no longer recognizable in the theatre, and that he withholds the true subject of the play – religious experience – from the audience as long as possible, using the most elaborate disguises to woo the spectator and establish verisimilitude in a realistic style. Thus where Cocteau and Giraudoux see the stage as a place to show things Eliot sees it as a place to imitate reality and suggest things. *The Family Reunion* remains his strongest verse play because at least it does what he wants in verse, but when Eliot worried about 'a failure of adjustment between the Greek story and the modern situation' (*On Poetry and Poets*, p. 84) he confused the issue. What matters first in the theatre is boldness. Myth is useless because, as Steiner observes, what was the expression of a complete and traditional image of life which allowed the poet to achieve, immediately, terror or delight from a shared habit of belief no longer has that power and can exist only as a footnote in the programme. Myths are not merely dead; they are, which is worse from a theatrical point of view, literary. Eliot's Furies look thin in a modern light because of this loss but if they had been less furtive and foreign they might have passed in a theatrical light. And they are crucial; moving them off-stage destroys the meaning of the play since they must be transformed. Agatha steps into the embrasure to become the shining ones but if they have only been figments of Harry's imagination (not to mention the other people in the play who see the ghosts) how can she be transformed and into what?

After *Murder in the Cathedral* Eliot refused to write any more historical or religious plays. He wished to write verse for characters living more or less the same life as members of the audience though he hoped that 'our own sordid, dreary daily world would be suddenly illuminated and transfigured' (*On Poetry and Poets*, p. 82). By most people's standards the lives of characters in Eliot's plays seem far from sordid. They exhibit the upper-middle class elegance of their source, a Coward comedy of manners, an obvious choice, but one, like all realistic surfaces, susceptible to dating. The new play was finished in 1937 (its seed lies in the epigraph to *Sweeney*) and *The Family Reunion* was Eliot's most undisguisedly versified verse drama. His letters show him urgently grappling with the problems of the theatre: witness a note to E. Martin Browne on the use of naked lights on the stage, as on birthday cakes. It is a pity that Gielgud and his impressive cast never materialized, but Michael Redgrave took the part of the hero, Harry, who returns to Wishwood for his mother's birthday heavy with guilt at the thought that he might have pushed his wife off the deck of an ocean liner and haunted by the Furies. The family tangle includes two brothers who have car accidents which were more dramatic then than now and which bring in the police and add to the suspense; but Eliot is aiming at something more than an Agatha Christie play:

> What we have written is not a story of detection,
> Of crime and punishment, but of sin and expiation.
> It is possible that you have not known what sin
> You shall expiate, or whose, or why. It is certain
> That the knowledge of it must precede the expiation.

By the end of the play the various characters are sorted out, the mother is dead, Harry will leave his estate to his brother and go away (to be a missionary it is hinted) and the final scene shows Agatha and Mary stalking round the lighted birthday cake. There is a lot of choral speaking, very much in the 'what shall we do in this modern world' vein, and though the intermittent power of the play is undeniable the choice of naturalism, given the subject of the play, was not happy. Eliot was interested in the supernatural not the natural and the result is not the unified form he achieved in *Murder in the Cathedral* but a naturalistic action which lapses into devices: arias, duets, choruses and ·invocations. Remarkable as the verse frequently is it cannot overcome this split and, as Ronald Gaskell observes

> the natural world is left to establish itself through the physical presence of actors and since there is no significant physical action this world is simply not made real to us; how therefore could the play show the interpenetration of supernatural on natural?
>
> (*Drama and Reality*, p. 138)

However the imagery is given the task, here, of revealing thought or spiritual experience which is the stuff of the play and not decoration. The play was revived in 1956 by Peter Brook when it was still considered an acquired taste.

The Second World War intervened before the next play, *One-Eyed Riley* – a comedy – was performed at the Edinburgh Festival with E. Martin Browne established as Eliot's producer. Reading his account we can see Eliot's lack of confidence in himself as a dramatist for commercial theatre. Verse, and poetry, is sacrificed to dramatic utility but it never seems to be Eliot's idea of dramatic utility. He was tackling an unholy trade which is no job for the fastidious, and trying to bring forth a new verse drama would sap the confidence of anyone. In *The Cocktail Party*, as the play was eventually called, Eliot turned the drawing-room comedy of manners, a comfortable, familiar form into a look at the spiritual life, though noticeably the saints and martyrs recede and ordinary life comes to the forefront. If the play's lineage is Hawthorne's *The Marble Faun* and James's

The Wings of the Dove the obvious foster-parents were Euripides and Coward. The curtain rises on a party given by Edward Chamberlayne whose wife has just left him and who has not been able to prevent all the guests from coming, including an Unidentified Guest. The chatter about a joke (no tigers), Lady Klootz and the wedding cake or Delia Verinder and her three (?) brothers, and the business of where Lavinia's aunt actually lives needs no verse and would be better in straightforward dialogue by Coward or Wilde. The discussion between the Unidentified Guest and Edward which probes his relationship with Lavinia is in verse which is useful if we have become interested in characters rather than the plot. The various guests return on various pretexts which is both funny and, on second thoughts, rather sinister. In Act II the Unidentified Guest turns out to be Sir Henry Harcourt-Reilly and Edward discovers that as he had been having an affair with Celia his wife had been having an affair with Peter. The sin, as in all Eliot's work, is isolation:

> What is hell? Hell is oneself,
> Hell is alone, the other figures in it
> Merely projections.

> (*The Cocktail Party*, p. 99)

This is not merely Eliot's answer to the Sartre of *Huis Clos*, it is a conviction that runs through the play. Thus Celia comments:

> No. I mean that what has happened has made me aware
> That I've always been alone. That one always is alone.
> Not simply the ending of one relationship,
> Not even simply finding that it never existed –
> But a revelation about my relationship
> With *everybody*. Do you know –
> It no longer seems worth while to *speak* to anyone

> (*The Cocktail Party*, p. 133)

The team of Good Samaritans under Sir Henry offer choices:

> The best of a bad job is all any of us make of it –
> Except of course, the saints –
>
> *(The Cocktail Party*, p. 126)

So what is the good life? Some

> Maintain themselves by the common routine,
> Learn to avoid excessive expectation,
> Become tolerant of themselves and others,
> Giving and taking, in the usual actions
> Where there is to give and take.

But Celia chooses the sanatorium and the Act ends with a libation which is odd even in Harley Street.

The Third Act opens two years later when the Chamberlaynes are giving another party. The exchange between Lavinia and the Caterer's man is necessary but hardly in verse; indeed the verse works very well for a description of Celia's crucifixion but even for Peter's chatter it seems inappropriate:

> I flew over from New York last night –
> I left Los Angeles three days ago.
> I saw Sheila Paisley at lunch today
> And she told me you were giving a party –
> She's coming on later, after the Gunnings –
> So I said, I really must crash in:
> It's my only chance to see Edward and Lavinia.
> I'm only over for a week, you see,
> And I'm driving down to the country this evening,
> So I knew you wouldn't mind my looking in so early.
> It does seem ages since I last saw any of you!
> And how are you Alex? And dear old Julia!
>
> *(The Cocktail Party*, p. 164)

Once more the characters have been sorted out: Celia has been crucified, Peter can make films and the Chamberlaynes can give their party. Brooks Atkinson, reviewing the play in 1950, deplored the fact that it was insufficiently poetic and thought it needed 'more eloquence, passion and imaginative courage' while T. C. Worsley, reviewing the second production in 1956, remarked that telling the audience that the verse was unobtrusive was hardly the strongest recommendation for verse drama. It may be actable language but it is verse of the surface (though, as Raymond Williams points out, not superficial: *Drama from Ibsen to Brecht*, p. 190) and Eliot works so hard to keep it that, not to shatter the illusion of a West End drawing room, that the interpenetration between that room and the life of the saint never takes place. Instead of tension we have compromise. We are not surprised that Eliot found it more difficult to write verse for Alex than for Celia since that is the nub of the problem for modern verse drama. And it is hard to resist the feeling that the ordinary life (if cocktail parties are ordinary life) and the way of beatitude are totally discrete, and a suspicion that what we are witnessing is a sort of secret society kind of Christianity (Alex has connections even in California); while the verse seems to be used to trap Christian reality in a humdrum quasi-prosaic secular world (see William Arrowsmith, 'The Comedy of T. S. Eliot', *Modern Drama*, pp. 143–51).

After this play there is what Raymond Williams describes as a radical loss of substance: Eliot choosing the sociable way – 'but he was never, in any case, very sociable' (*Modern Tragedy*, 1966, p. 166). *The Confidential Clerk* (1953) is clearly comedy and may be farce, and if its source is Euripides the midwife was Oscar Wilde. Sir Claude Mulhammer is about to introduce his son Colby Simpkins as confidential clerk to his wife Lady Elizabeth (though Colby would prefer to be a musician as Sir Claude had wanted to be a potter), who has already taken a dislike to another illegitimate child, Lucasta Angel and her fiancé B. Kaghan and who has herself also mislaid a son when the father was killed by a rhinoceros in Tanganyika. They are helped to sort things out by Eggerson, the former confidential clerk, who is also a vicar's warden and a keen gardener which, like

Lady Elizabeth's interest in the Wisdom of the East, helps to introduce religious ideas. But mainly what interests us is the thickening of the plot when Lady Elizabeth claims that Colby is her son and the nurse, Mrs Guzzard, is sent for. Thus everyone begins to find out what the good life for each should be rather than what others expect of them. Lucasta announces her engagement to B. Kaghan who as Barnabas turns out to be Lady Elizabeth's son, while Colby is really Mrs Guzzard's son (with a father who was a failed musician) and not Sir Claude's. So Eggerson can find Colby a job as an organist prior to his going into holy orders. It is difficult to hear what is in verse or not. As in previous plays the choice is between ordinary family life and the dedicated life leading away from the family, but there are no set speeches, arias and such-like, only what Donoghue describes as *sostenuto* (*The Third Voice*, p. 139). E. Martin Browne claims that Eliot's aim was to make people forget they were listening to verse and most reviewers agreed that it was non-detectable. Art replaces Beatitude which means that the audience can understand it and yet recognize the special quality which allows a jump to higher things. It is all sleight-of-hand and even D. E. Jones allows it to be 'only just across the border from prose'.

The Elder Statesman (1958) marked a return to tragedy though its tone was probably mellowed by the poet's marriage to Valerie Fletcher in 1957. The 'story' seems to be that of *The Family Reunion* once more. Lord Claverton has retired and is dying and though his daughter Monica is in love with Charles she cannot leave her father who has a horror of being left alone. He is not alone for long since he is visited by Fred Culverwell (now Gomez) and reminded of the time when he ran over a man (who was dead) and did not stop the car, and when he arrives at Badgley Court he meets Mrs Carghill (who was Maisie Montjoy, a former mistress bought off by his father). His own son Michael, although he has not run over any corpses or got any girls pregnant, is tired of being his father's son and accepts a job abroad offered him by Gomez and Mrs Carghill. This solves Michael's problem but naturally worries his father. Lord Claverton's verse even when he is confessing everything is seldom warm or spirited and even his moment of truth would lose nothing if printed in prose, particularly as prose could carry the sparse lines of imagery in the play:

> I cannot bar his way, as you know very well.
> Michael's a free agent. So if he chooses
> To place himself in your power, Fred Culverwell,
> Of his own volition to contract his enslavement,
> I cannot prevent him. I have something to say to you,
> Michael, before you go. I shall never repudiate you
> Though you repudiate me. I see now clearly
> The many mistakes I have made
> My whole life through, mistake upon mistake,
> The mistaken attempts to correct mistakes
> By methods which proved to be equally mistaken.
> I see that your mother and I, in our failure
> To understand each other, both misunderstood you
> In our divergent ways. When I think of your childhood,
> When I think of the happy little boy who was Michael,
> When I think of your boyhood and adolescence,
> And see how all the efforts aimed at your good
> Only succeeded in defeating each other,
> How can I feel anything but sorrow and compunction?
>
> (*The Elder Statesman*, p. 99)

It is true that the lovers come together at the end of the play in a warmer sort of verse but, as Tynan remarked, the images of the play evoke only 'well-bred dread' and, in spite of Sophocles, *The Elder Statesman* remains Pinero on stilts (*Tynan on Theatre*, p. 78). The problem may be that the spiritual life is lacking in action and action is the lifeblood of the theatre, and for Eliot the spiritual life is both theme and subject. In an interview in 1949 Eliot was suggesting that it was time to turn to Theatre of Character rather than Theatre of Ideals (quoted D. E. Jones, p. 205), possibly a recognition that the dramatist might persuade more through flesh and blood than myth or verse.

Eliot said that he wished to produce ordinary plays written by a Christian rather than plays with an overtly Christian purpose; that, as in his poetry, he wished to reject the romantic and the spurious, to unfold the life of the spirit. But it seems that when he does achieve things that one would have thought only prose could achieve his success is hampered by the fact that he is writing in verse. Lavinia, in *The Cocktail Party*, says that she would love to hear Sir Henry speaking poetry – 'if it answers my question'. The challenge to the obvious, superficial and naturalistic drama was welcome, and Eliot's belief that a craving for poetic drama is permanent in human nature (*Selected Essays*, p. 56) is probably true. But only a poet would have assumed that such drama must be in verse.

5
Christopher Fry

Tynan wrote that where Eliot anoints Fry gilds ('Prose and the Playwright', *Tynan on Theatre*, pp. 329–35) and if Fry's success shows that there was a welcome for verse on the British stage it also shows that Eliot was wise in recognizing the dangers as well as fearing the prejudice. T. S. Eliot wished to say something and it was important that he be listened to rather than that he charmed audiences with pretty words. Tynan was concerned in his review to defend prose from the attack of verse drama which, in 1954, seemed a real attack, but other critics echo his complaints. Eric Bentley, for example, complains that Fry has been constructing a polemic against realism which was seen as an obstacle to beauty, yet Fry's beauty 'is too calculated an effect ... which the author seems to be forever congratulating himself on'. This comment, significantly, occurs in a review of Chekhov's *The Three Sisters* where great beauty is achieved with the least strain and most abundance (*What is Theatre?*, pp. 221–4). Certainly Fry's statements do strive to become a theory of drama. In a talk that reads like a manifesto, in *The Listener* (1950), Fry said:

> Poetry is the language in which man explores his own amazement. It is the language in which he says heaven and earth in one word. It is the language in which he speaks of himself and his predicament as though for the first time ... And, if you accept my proposition that reality is altogether different from our stale view of it, we can say that poetry is the language of reality.

Denis Donoghue has rightly challenged the easy notions and the glib use of words like 'reality' but his analyses of the plays (chapter 11, *The Third Voice*) are not merely unsympathetic – for a book devoted to verse drama – they seem to take little note of the theatrical context. Can, one wonders, Mr Donoghue have ever sat through *The Elder Statesman*? Donoghue feels that Fry's reputation as a dramatist 'is one of the more disquieting facts about the contemporary theatre'(*The Third Voice*, p. 180), that the comedies up to *The Dark is Light Enough* 'can point to nothing apart from their tenuous and precious selves; that is what their style is, pervadingly self-regarding' (ibid., p. 182) and that when Fry has purged his language of excess in that play a heavily sentimental tone creeps in to offend Mr Donoghue, who concludes that Fry's permanent contribution to the theatre is likely to be slight and not very interesting.

Most critics agree that the language is decorative, that it blurs character differentiation (and that the characters are verbal puppets anyway), that the plays are badly constructed and lack seriousness, and that when Fry pruned them of verbal indulgence they became colourless, which is fatal in the theatre. The early plays, however, demand attention if to the wrong things. But in whose judgement are certain things absolutely wrong? As Geoffrey Bullough points out *The Lady's Not For Burning* may have been poetry for the West End (Gielgud's phrase) but perhaps the West End needed poetry as much as anywhere else? The controversy over Eliot and Fry is now history and, in retrospect, trivial history. Fry has his champion in Derek Stanford, whose British Council Pamphlet no. 54 and an appreciation published in 1951 (revised 1952) represent an attempt to endow Fry with importance. Unfortunately Mr Stanford chooses to claim for the plays a philosophical undercurrent, a high seriousness which misses the fun of the plays as surely as Fry lacked stamina for drama. At a point in time Fry reinstated the comic spirit into verse drama which had been a gloomy matter and challenged the belief that audiences were afraid of language.

Stanford has a point when he suggests that Fry offered mystery instead of a deterministic universe and verse instead of the naturalistic language of the stage. He bridged that gap between realist plays of commercial theatre and literary verse drama as few other writers have done. Fry's remark that what we had gained in verisimilitude we had lost in truth ('Poetry and the Theatre', *Adam*, 1951) has more than a grain of perception in it and it is a theatrical kind of perception.

Fry was not a poet coming into the theatre. Born of religious parents (he is as religious a dramatist as Eliot) he moved from teaching into repertory theatre and back to teaching until his appointment in 1934 as director of Tunbridge Wells Repertory Players. He wrote the Festival Play *The Boy with a Cart* in 1937 and moved in 1940 to the post of director of the Oxford Playhouse to which he returned after the war finishing, with the help of Charles Williams, his tragedy *The Firstborn* (1946) for performance outside Tewkesbury Abbey. The play tells of the captivity of the Jews under Pharaoh and their escape led by Moses who is horrified to discover that freedom entails the sacrifice of his nephew-by-adoption, Rameses:

MOSES I do not know why the necessity of God
        Should feed on grief; but it seems so. And to know it
        Is not to grieve less, but to see grief grow big
        With what has died, and in some spirit differently
        Bear it back to life. The blame could impale me
        For ever; I could be so sick of heart
        That who asked for my life should have it; or I could
          see
        Man's life go forward only by guilt and guilt.
        Then we should always be watching Rameses die.
        Whereas he had such life his death can only
        Take him for a moment, to undo his mortality,
        And he is here pursuing the ends of the world.
ANATH You have nothing now except the wilderness.

MOSES The wilderness has wisdom.
      And what does eternity bear witness to
      If not at last to hope?

                    (*Three Plays*, p. 94)

In the same mould *Thor, With Angels* was performed at the Chapter House in Canterbury, and *A Sleep of Prisoners* (1951) at the University Church in Oxford: plays which also see sacrifice as a requirement of life which is being

    'in a sort of a universe and a bit of a fix.
    It's what they call flesh we're in.
    And a fine old dance it is'.

But Fry is principally important for his comedies in the commercial theatre. His first, *A Phoenix Too Frequent*, was performed at the Mercury Theatre in 1946 and introduced Fry to London as a dramatist rather than as a man who wrote plays for special occasions. Yet in one sense it was a play for a special occasion: 1946. As Fry admits he had the story from Jeremy Taylor who had it from Petronius. Dynamene and her reluctant servant propose to stay with the body of her husband Virilius until they too die but a soldier, Tegeus, guarding six corpses of criminals near the tomb intervenes and Dynamene falls in love with him. But Tegeus returns to find one of his corpses is missing which is itself a hanging matter so, to save Tegeus, Dynamene offers him the body of Virilius:

                He has no further use
    For what he left of himself to lie with us here.
    Is there any reason why he should't hang
    On your holly tree? Better, far better, he,
    Than you who are still alive, and surely better
    Than *idling* into corruption?
TEGEUS   Hang your husband?
    Dynamene, it's terrible, horrible.
DYNAMENE How little you understand. I loved

His life not his death. And now we can give his
  death
The power of life. Not horrible; wonderful!
Isn't it so! That I should be able to feel
He moves again in the world, accomplishing
Our welfare? It's more than my grief could do.
  (*Four Modern Verse Plays*, Penguin, pp. 137–8)

The play was revived at the Arts Theatre where *The Lady's
Not For Burning* was produced in 1948.

Fry has a special belief in the power of comedy:

The bridge by which we cross from tragedy to comedy and
back again is precarious and narrow. We find ourselves in
one or the other by the turn of a thought; a turn such as
we make when we turn from speaking to listening. I know
that when I set about writing a comedy the idea presents
itself to me first of all as tragedy ... Somehow the characters
have to unmortify themselves: to affirm life and assimilate
death and persevere in joy. Their hearts must be as deter-
mined as the phoenix; what burns must also light and renew.
  ('Comedy', *Theatre in the Twentieth Century*, edited
        R. W. Corrigan, New York, pp. 111–13)

There are times when, according to Fry, comedy is especially
important

and the present is one of them: time when the loudest faith
has been faith in a trampling materialism, when literature
has been thought unrealistic which did not mark and remark
our poverty and doom. Joy (of a kind) has been all on the
devil's side, and one of the necessities of our time is to
redeem it.

To achieve this redemption Fry proposed a comedy of seasons,
four comedies of mood in each of which 'the scene, the season,
and the characters, are bound together in one climate'. ('*Venus*
Considered', *Theatre News-Letter*, 1950). If this is to be success-

ful then the verse ought to sound differently from play to play but as most critics observe (and, for example, Raymond Williams has demonstrated) April *sounds* just like November!

The Lady's Not For Burning was the spring play, full of April showers, tears and catarrh and however slight it may strike us now it was exactly right for a tired, post-war world. Its assertion, like Dynamene's of life, colour, splendid language and remarkable acting was most welcome in a drab world. And the acting was remarkable, for Fry's plays were plays for star performers like Gielgud, Olivier and Edith Evans. Since verse was there as the deliberate opposite of prose it could be stressed, enjoyed and exploited. Most of the characters talk alike because they are all trying to outshine one another in verbal cleverness but since this is basically a comedy of situation the development of character was less important than it would be were seriousness (and dramatic involvement) intended. Even so, if we listen to the play, it does say something:

> THOMAS Your innocence is on at such a rakish angle
> It gives you quite an air of iniquity.
> By the most naked of compassionate angels
> Hadn't you better answer that bell? With a mere
> Clouding of your unoccupied eyes, madam,
> Or the twitch of the neck: what better use can we put
> Our faces to than to have them express kindness
> While we're thinking of something else? Oh, be dis-
>   turbed,
> Be disturbed, madam, to the extent of a tut
> And I will thank God for civilization.
> This is my last throw, my last poor gamble
> On the human heart.
>
> (*The Lady's Not For Burning*, pp. 12–13)

In his own light way Fry is asking the audience to pay attention just as in 1948 Arthur Miller, in more sombre fashion .was saying: Pay attention. The need to work out problems rather

than die is a theme of the play. The opening word is 'Soul'
balanced by the accounts for plastering up a draught in the
privy. The hero is a world-weary soldier returning from the
wars whose quest for death is cluttered up with the wooing of
Alizon and a witch-hunt, all of which confirm his sense of the
damnation of the world but also issue forth in love and laughter:

THOMAS ... For God's sake, shall we laugh?
JENNET   For what reason?
THOMAS For the reason of laughter, since laughter is surely
    The surest touch of genius in creation.
    Would *you* ever have thought of it, I ask you,
    If you had been making man, stuffing him full
    Of such hopping greeds and passions that he had
    To blow himself to pieces as often as he
    Conveniently can manage it – would it also
    Have occurred to you to make him burst himself
    With such a phenomenon as cachinnation?
    That same laughter, madam, is an irrelevancy
    Which almost amounts to revelation.

(ibid., p. 50)

Obviously we cannot insist on a dark metaphysical side to the
play. The rustic is discovered, and the world is unchanged.
Thomas remarks that metaphor is a wonderful thing but it can
merely beguile. The play, like *The Crucible*, is about a witch-
hunt but the mob is kept in its place – mainly off-stage – and
when it enters it is as a comic character. Thus we are left with
a graceful, fantastic play which is enjoyable.

Clearly there must be some progress and Fry's second play,
Venus Observed, shows hints at character-drawing. This is the
autumn play – 'a house beginning to fall into decay, the characters, most of them, are in middle life' – and it is another comedy
of situation. An ageing Duke wishes his son Edgar to choose
a bride for him from three old relationships. Then his agent's
daughter, Perpetua, turns up and both the Duke and Edgar

contend for her. But the agent, Reedbeck, has been swindling the Duke to the horror of his son, Dominic, so Perpetua had better marry the Duke to keep it in the family. This strange household also employs an ex-burglar and an ex-liontamer. One of the other contenders for the Duke, Rosabel, sets fire to the observatory from which the Duke and Perpetua are rescued (the ex-burglar is good with ladders) and so Perpetua will marry Edgar, and the Duke Rosabel (when she comes out of prison). The verse is amusing but as T. C. Worsley pointed out there is a law of diminishing returns. Fry's reliance on words seems less astonishing a second time and when the language is more easily accepted the question arises: what is he doing with it? The decorations here have so little to do with what is being done that Worsley warned the dramatist he might not get away much longer 'with this line of patter' (*The Fugitive Art*, pp. 116, 118).

The next play, for winter, produced a certain chill and some attempt at inner poetry in less florid verse. *The Dark is Light Enough* (produced in 1954 by Peter Brook with décor by Messel and Edith Evans as the Countess Rosmarin) concerns events at the chateau of the Countess during the Hungarian revolution against the Empire in 1848–9. The Countess has friends on both sides and gives shelter indiscriminately – even to Richard Gettner who was married to her daughter and who nearly alienates that daughter from her present husband Count Peter. We are told

> how apparently undemandingly
> She moves among us; and yet
> Lives make and unmake themselves in her neighbourhood
> As nowhere else. There are many names I could name
> Who would have been remarkably otherwise
> Except for her divine non-interference.
>
> (*The Dark is Light Enough*, pp. 4–5)

The difficulty is that whatever her behaviour achieves, which is obscure, being perfect she cannot develop or surprise us very much and resembles, in Tynan's words, a 'benignly crinolined soup-kitchen'.

A gap followed this play, although Fry was translating Anouilh and Giraudoux, until 1961 when *Curtmantle* appeared, using both verse and prose as in *The Boy With A Cart*. This was not the expected summer comedy but a sort of dream pageant, possibly influenced by his film work about Henry II. In Act I Becket becomes archbishop, is assassinated in Act II and in Act III Henry does penance. But the play is also about Henry's struggle with others: his queen Eleanor, his sons and the barons and his hope of creating 'a secure Plantagenet empire/And a government of justice'. Fry claimed that he was writing a serious play and not looking at history, like Eliot, through a stained-glass window. His portrait of the king is part of a look at the interplay of laws – civil, canon, moral, aesthetic and divine – and how they belong or do not belong to one another (Preface, pp. viii–ix). The verse is frankly serviceable with occasional flashes of the old style, as when Eleanor on being told that the French king's prayers for a son have been answered, much to Henry's chagrin, remarks:

> When heaven makes one of its rare rejoinders
> I should have thought it the merest common civility
> For all of us to attempt a smile.

But when we listen to the play and then, for example, to Whiting's *Marching Song*, it is the latter which sounds more like verse than prose.

There was no new play from Fry until 1970, the year when he was also translating *Peer Gynt* for the Chichester Festival, an occupation which is more encouraging than film scripts. So, nine years after *Curtmantle*, the last comedy of the seasons appeared, *A Yard of Sun*. This summer play is, for the first time, about modern times (i.e. 1946) though it takes place in Sienna, on the eve of the Palio. The yard of sun is a short period (summer is not a way of life but something to be enjoyed) and a small space. Into the Palazzo which Bruno takes care of, just after the war, come hope and the residual guilt and suspicion that come from war. Angelino Bruno has three sons: Roberto who was a partisan and is now a doctor with strong social principles, Luigi who was a Blackshirt and now reports football matches for a local paper and Edmondo, the black sheep of the family who returns from being a profiteer in Portugal a millionaire. Edmondo, with his wife, proposes to help the family. This arrival is intertwined with the story of Alfio who has come to ride in the Palio because he needs money for his sick mother, and who is looking for his father Cesare who lived with Bruno's neighbour Giosetta by whom he had a daughter, Grazie. Alfio learns that his father was betrayed and taken away. Cesare returns, too, and it is revealed that he was accidentally betrayed by his daughter. Luigi's horse wins the Palio (without Luigi on him), Cesare will return to his wife and son, Roberto will marry Grazie, and Ana Clara leaves with her husband Edmondo. Bruno turns down the chance of opening the Palazzo as a restaurant: in short nothing has changed, after the heat of the Palio things return to what they should be.

The verse is once more serviceable but Benedict Nightingale, in his review for the *New Statesman*, printed a piece of prose from Pinter's *The Homecoming* side by side with a piece of verse from this play pointing out that the piece in prose is poetry whereas the piece in verse is prose. The example from Fry is wickedly chosen but it makes the point that dramatic poetry has very little to do with verse these days; the contemporary prose may not be Jacobean gold but it lifts language to levels Fry fails to reach. Nightingale objects once more that the language is not matched with strongly felt themes or developing characters. The play is about optimism but explores none of the motives or actions which should go to substantiate that mood. Fry has certainly made attempts to be idiomatic, even colloquial, but again the setting allows for an Italian opera. We are not listening to the man in the street, only to a man in a Sienese street, on a hot day when the Palio is imminent.

Of course Fry has always stoutly maintained that the language of the streets is not everything, however brilliantly recorded:

> It is an instrument which reflects the full life of man, and if we let it dwindle we dwindle with it. But apart from the utilitarian question of language, I believe the need for poetry is an essential part of the human condition. Audiences, if they trust themselves to it, take to it readily. Do you think that when speech in the theatre gets closer to speech in the street we necessarily get closer to the nature of man? Surely, the business of the theatre is an exploration of that nature, so that the listener can perhaps be aware of more about himself. At present we concentrate mainly on behaviour; but isn't it important to try and find out *purpose*, to know what we're driving for?
>
> (*Twentieth Century*, February 1961, vol. 169, 1008, p. 190)

Poetry may be an essential part of the human condition but is verse? John Arden, confessing a literary first-love for Fry, suggests that he has a great gift for language but not much else. He does not marry that language to a strong situation and he uses images when he wants to rather than keeping them for the moments when nothing else would be suitable. Arden believes this is inefficient in the theatre where a play should work at first sitting but still encourage people to see it again because it has hinted at a richness which merits a second visit.

It was not verse which made Fry successful; and that success was temporary because he never evolved into strong subjects and language that was more than platitude and decoration. That was not the fault of verse. We do not wish to banish the luxury of language from the theatre but, as Tynan reminds us, we must lose the idea that it is incompatible with prose. Poets of our modern theatre will, it is safe to say, use this new, flexible and shining instrument.

6
Poets of the Theatre

Writing in verse was essentially a writer's reform which produced both a sense of the unnatural in the audience and a conflict of conventions in performance. As Raymond Williams points out in *Drama in Performance* (Pelican, 1972) the verse was evidence of one convention where action, movement and design were part of another so that the actor speaking verse was still moving and behaving in a naturalistic way. It may also be true that the abuses of language that concern George Steiner, by political terror, the illiteracy of mass consumption and the mass media, have weakened the idea that words are the mystery at the source of tragic poetry, while those same mass media, the cinema and television, have certainly relegated words to the position of sub-titles to pictures. As Ibsen predicted, the best plays of this century have all been in prose and the attack on naturalistic drama from verse drama was brief, but it prepared the way for more striking challenges in European theatre: Beckett and Brecht.

Beckett belongs firmly to that French tradition which rejected language as firmly as it rejected plot and character, the ingredients of the well-made play and yet, paradoxically, succeeded in writing drama. The rejection of language was, of course, thematic rather than actual and produced some striking results as the following extract from *Waiting for Godot* illustrates:

ESTRAGON In the meantime let's try and converse calmly, since we're incapable of keeping silent.

VLADIMIR You're right, we're inexhaustible.

ESTRAGON It's so we won't think.

VLADIMIR We have that excuse.

ESTRAGON It's so we won't hear.

VLADIMIR We have our reasons.

ESTRAGON All the dead voices.

VLADIMIR They make a noise like wings.

ESTRAGON Like leaves.

VLADIMIR Like sand.

ESTRAGON Like leaves.

Silence

VLADIMIR They all speak together.

ESTRAGON Each one to itself.

Silence

VLADIMIR Rather they whisper.

ESTRAGON They rustle.

VLADIMIR They murmur.

ESTRAGON They rustle.

Silence

VLADIMIR What do they say?

ESTRAGON They talk about their lives.

VLADIMIR To have lived is not enough for them.

ESTRAGON They have to talk about it.

VLADIMIR To be dead is not enough for them.

ESTRAGON It is not sufficient.

Silence

VLADIMIR They make a noise like feathers.

ESTRAGON Like leaves.

VLADIMIR Like ashes.

ESTRAGON Like leaves.

Long silence

VLADIMIR Say something!
ESTRAGON I'm trying.

> *Long silence*

(Waiting for Godot, pp. 62–3)

Here we can see what A. Alvarez means when he writes of the 'combination of austerity straining against imaginative wealth' that makes this as much a poem in its own right as part of a poetic drama:

> Eliot had seemed to be opening new ground in *Sweeney Agonistes*, but he abandoned the project; in his later plays, despite his absorption in the technical problem of breaking up the traditional iambic pentameter, he managed to do little more than add a dimension of spiritual portentousness to the world of Terence Rattigan. Beckett seems far less grandiose ... but he ends with plays that are genuinely poetic, both in dramatic conception and in language; they make their effect like poems, immediately and elliptically, through a language which is at once stripped to its essentials and yet continually stirring with life.
>
> (Beckett, London, 1973, pp. 84–5; cf. Martin Esslin,
The Theatre of the Absurd, 1974, p. 38)

While it is possible to recognize the verbal merit of the passage its full effect occurs only in context; this is dialogue which calls for the ears but it also demands the eyes, fulfilling Artaud's ideal of total theatre.

On the British stage Pinter is Beckett's cousin and there is a similar duet in *The Birthday Party* when Goldberg and McCann interrogate Stanley. But again dialogue out of context only accounts for part of the effect of the play. Pinter's dialogue, much more than Beckett's, is that which could be spoken by ordinary people in ordinary situations and yet the final impression is one of being just beyond the edge of ordinariness, which allows a name like Kafka to slip into critical discussion. Take any speech from the early plays – say *The Caretaker* – and you have what Ibsen asked for: poetic creation in the plain, un-varnished speech of reality. Pinter's strength, as M. C. Brad-brook has pointed out (*English Dramatic Form*, London, 1965), lies in the precision and control of rhythm in the speech of his inarticulate characters. The effect is poetic but the speech belongs to an oral tradition; the words must be spoken not read. It is what John Russell Taylor has called 'orchestrated' naturalism:

> Far more than the fantasticated verse plays of Christopher Fry and his followers, or the verse-in-disguise plays of T. S. Eliot, his works are the true poetic drama of our time, for he alone understood that poetry in the theatre is not achieved merely by couching ordinary sentiments in an elaborately artificial poetic diction, like Fry, or writing what is formally verse but not appreciable to the unwarned ear as anything but prose, like Eliot.
>
> (*Anger and After*, p. 358)

Thus dialogue is part of a whole and as such may, in isolation seem to mean very little, as in this characteristic duet from David Storey's *Home*:

JACK   *sits:* You do any fighting?
HARRY What?
JACK   Army.
HARRY Oh, well, then ... modest amount.
JACK   Nasty business.
HARRY Oh! Doesn't bear thinking about.
JACK   Two relatives of mine killed in the war.
HARRY Oh dear.
JACK   You have to give thanks, I must say.
HARRY Oh, yes.
JACK   Mother's father ... a military man.
HARRY Yes.
JACK   All his life.

HARRY He must have seen some sights.

JACK Oh, yes.

HARRY Must have all had meaning then.

JACK Oh, yes. India, Africa. He's buried as a matter of fact in Hong Kong.

HARRY Really?

JACK So they tell me. Never been there myself.

HARRY No.

JACK Hot climates, I think, can be the very devil if you haven't the temperament.

HARRY Huh! You don't have to tell me.

JACK Been there?

HARRY No, no. Just what one reads.

JACK Dysentery.

HARRY Beriberi.

JACK Yellow fever.

HARRY Oh dear.

JACK As well, of course, as all the other contingencies.

HARRY Oh yes.

JACK At times one's glad simply to live on an island.

HARRY Yes.

(*Home*, pp. 19–20)

Language in the theatre, as John Russell Brown has rather exhaustively demonstrated,[1] is not just words, it is silences, pauses, gestures, movements and patterns on the stage. Increasingly since the Second World War actors (and audiences) have begun to respond consciously to the sub-text as well as to the text – that is to recognize what is being said beneath what is being spoken – a practice usually traced to Chekhov and particularly as produced by Stanislavski.

Beckett and Absurd drama restored those possibilities to the theatre which the verse dramatists had been insisting on, affirming that man is not to be defined solely in terms of psychology

[1] See John Russell Brown, *Theatre Language*, London, 1972.

and environment, but is also a poetic and metaphysical being. Verse drama had called attention to the drabness of language and the superficial nature of the action but basically Eliot's plays were Rattigan with spiritual portentousness which is still Rattigan. Discontent with the language and action of the theatre go hand in hand, parts of a recognition that what the theatre was doing had become largely irrelevant to life on the streets outside in the 1950s. *Saint's Day* (1951) by John Whiting was an abortive start, puzzling audiences too much, but *Waiting for Godot* (1955) became enough of a fashion to compel audiences to see it. The real start to change was in 1956 when the Berliner Ensemble came to England and, more significantly, the English Stage Company opened at the Royal Court Theatre. It was one of their early productions, *Look Back in Anger*, which almost accidentally marked the new beginning because it found an audience. Where Eliot and Fry had, as Laurence Kitchin puts it, built up a respectable circulation in cathedrals and training colleges but remained on the margins of public taste this play tapped sources of widespread resentment (*Mid-Century Drama*, 1966, p. 59). It spoke, according to T. C. Worsley, with 'the authentic new tone of the 1950s, desperate, savage, resentful and, at times, very funny' (quoted *Anger and After*, p. 31). In retrospect it may only have been Pinero with a lower-class accent, but Osborne intended to make people *feel* and this ability to move audiences, to shake them up, was something neither Eliot nor Fry had had. Osborne's rhetorical prose and angry passions suited the impure context of the stage where delicate lace cannot be seen and once the labels of Angry or Committed Theatre had peeled off, the tirades of Jimmy Porter are nearer Giraudoux than Brecht. These arias continue through most of Osborne's plays to harass the audience. Even Wesker, that most prosaic and committed of dramatists, is seen in plays like *The Four Seasons* and *The Friends* as parabolic rather than naturalistic. He, too, has come to orchestrate the words of his plays: witness his response to internal rhythms when producing the latter play (which is printed to show those rhythms). In the character of Macey he rejects the cliché of non-communication, that words act like dams; art and speech is the finding of 'the one right word which gives a solid shape to what before was only an intangible feeling. Words dams? They're gates, precious, magnificent – lovely!' (*The Friends*, pp. 21–2). As Wesker says realistic art is a contradiction in terms since art is the re-creation of experience not the copying of it.

But clearly the most obvious candidate as poet of the theatre in the conventional sense of poet as writer of verses would be John Arden, influenced by Masefield and Fry. In his speech to the NUS Festival at Leeds entitled 'Verse in the Theatre' (*New Theatre Magazine*, vol. 11, 3, April 1961, pp. 12–17) Arden agreed that there was only a limited place for verse in drama and doubted that plays could be written now in verse from beginning to end since whereas in Shakespeare it is the prose that stands out nowadays it would be verse. He himself uses verse but Pinter, who does not, manages by the use of repetition and elaboration to make his dialogue poetical if not metrical. Arden uses verse because he wishes to treat the material of the contemporary world in ballad form, using basic, simple situations painted in strong primary colours, though when verse is used it must be obviously verse as opposed to the surrounding prose and must never 'be allowed to droop into casual flaccidities' ('Telling a True Tale', *The Encore Reader*, p. 127). How this works can be seen in *Sergeant Musgrave's Dance* (1959) where the language is earthy with a rich north country flavour but cannot be labelled as naturalistic. As prose it is highly-charged rising at times into verse which, with the colours of the costumes and recurrent images, turns the basic parable into poetry of the theatre.

This is basically the Brechtian technique. Absurd drama had taken the walls with which naturalism enclosed the stage and transformed the drawing-room into the set for *Endgame* or one of Pinter's narrow rooms. It had attacked language, and particularly beautiful language, creating a theatre that existed in a whole situation: it was the culmination of a tradition that had grown sterile and imitative. As Martin Esslin recalls in *Brief Chronicles* (p. 37):

> Whatever their ideas, their social purpose, their political commitment may have been, the great naturalists Ibsen, Strindberg, Shaw, Hauptmann, Chekhov, Gorky, Schnitzler must ultimately be judged as great poets, poets of a new kind; they discovered the magic that lies behind the seemingly commonplace surface of ordinary life, the tragic greatness of simple people, the poetry of silences and reticences, the bitter ironies of unspoken thoughts ... poetry *of* the stage with an intensity and poignancy that could not have been achieved with the rules and methods of an earlier theatre, a poetry arising out of, and entirely in tune with, an industrialized, urbanized society and the image of man that, for better or for worse, it had created.

Beckett and other dramatists like him had recaptured that magic in one way, but Brecht chose another. In his 'Notes on a Folk Play' (*Brecht on Theatre*, translated John Willett, pp. 154–5) Brecht considers the two styles in the theatre: the elevated style worked out for great poetic masterpieces which can still be used if in a battered condition, and the second style, naturalistic, which has grown more and more feeble and compromised:

> All that has been provided by the elevated style is the unnaturalness and artificiality, the schematism and pompousness into whose depths this style tumbled before naturalism took over. And all that survives here of the great period of naturalism is the accidental, shapeless, unimaginative element which was part of naturalism even at its best. Thus new paths must be found. In what direction?

Clearly not verse drama, though verse and song are not excluded; and certainly not Absurd drama. But all three are kinds of revolt against the naturalistic stage and show a return to the more open stage. Where verse drama was only part of a convention, and Absurd drama was, by its basic premises, self-limiting and ultimately silent, Brecht and John Arden chose epic theatre which is arguably a whole convention. It is certainly the convention that most appeals to producers and it is they, rather than actors or writers, who have recently been the dominant force in the theatre. Indeed, Peter Brook and other great producers may very well rank among our poets of the theatre today.

7

Poetic Drama

We no longer have any excuse for feeling, as Peter Brook puts it, that 'a verse play is half-way between prose and opera, neither spoken nor sung, yet with a higher charge than prose – higher in content, higher somehow in moral value' (*the empty space*, p. 48). But the wheel of critical opinion has turned sufficiently to allow us to look at verse drama dispassionately and Katharine J. Worth, in *Revolutions in Modern English Drama* (1972), is able (chapter IV) to remind us just how experimental T. S. Eliot was. We can now see that verse drama in the 1940s served a useful function: it assisted at the birth of poetic drama and we should appreciate this and that by claiming for itself a higher moral value than prose the verse drew attention not merely to the language of the play but to the fact that some plays do have a higher moral charge than others. The period of the 1940s is too often lightly dismissed in favour of the heady days of 1956. John Russell Taylor in *Anger and After* (1969), writes that Fry's championship of verse in the theatre went more or less unsupported, and that the appeal of other verse drama was either merely modish or too parochial apart from those few dramatists who betook themselves to the radio. This is accurate but it is also grudging. The theatre of the 1940s had, appropriately, a talent to amuse which the theatre of the 1970s – when we are saturated with realism in the cinema and on television – might well return to, and its glories were not unappealing as Peter Brook reminds us:

... this was a theatre of colour and movement, of fine fabrics,

of shadows, of eccentric, cascading words, of leaps of thought
and of cunning machines, of lightness and of all forms of
mystery and surprise – it was a theatre of a battered Europe
that seemed to share one aim – a reaching back towards a
memory of lost grace.

(*the empty space*, p. 43)

The new poetic drama sounded less elegant, less facile, less
old-fashioned and seemed more relevant. Many of the best
dramatists writing after 1956 started their careers as actors –
John Osborne, Harold Pinter, Henry Livings, Charles Wood
– and it has had an effect on their writing. It must have
directed their attention to what happens in the theatre as well
as words. Verse dramatists, and particularly T. S. Eliot, were
misled into believing that the problem could be solved by finding
the right dramatic verse, overlooking the fact that a play is not
primarily a verbal medium: it is action, indicated by words and
gestures spoken by an actor – and the mind must be the focus
of attention not the words spoken. That is to say the words
spoken must lead directly to character and action and never stop
to admire themselves. The problem persists. Here is Peter
Barnes in his preface to *Leonardo's Last Supper*:

And so the aim is to create, by means of soliloquy, rhetoric,
formalized ritual, slapstick, songs and dances, a comic theatre
of contrasting moods and opposites, where everything is
simultaneously tragic and ridiculous.

Every play is a problem of language ... one had to find
... a live theatrical language which had the feel of a historical
period ... yet could be understood by a contemporary audience. This artificial vernacular had to have historical weight
yet be flexible enough to incorporate modern songs and
jokes. For such deliberate anachronisms can only work fully
if they spring out of an acceptable period texture. So I
pillaged everything, from Elizabethan argot to the Bible.

Barnes is no graverobber. He realized that language is a problem but he also accepts that the stage is a space to be filled; that drama hovers uncertainly between literature and spectacle. At the moment directors (many of whom work also in the cinema) want it to be mainly spectacle, something to look at – what Osborne has contemptuously called plays 'sort of about leaving nude girls in plastic bags at railway stations. Non verbal, you understand, no old words, just the maximum in participation' (*Time Present*, p. 46). This present time needs the useful reminder of verse drama that words count as much as scenery or even directors. They *are* difficult but ultimately they are all we have and we must use them – or how else shall we buy our ticket to get into the theatre?

Select Bibliography

The problem of verse drama in the twentieth century is part of the larger problem of what the modern theatre can or should do and any bibliography must reflect this. The obvious starting point is Denis Donoghue, *The Third Voice* (Princeton, 1966) which deals specifically with modern British and American verse drama, but readers will find George Steiner's *The Death of Tragedy* (London, 1961) very useful. Ronald Peacock attempts in *The Art of Drama* (London, 1957) to cope with an art form which belongs to both literature and the theatre; his *The Poet in the Theatre* (London, 1946, revised in 1960) grew out of a mood of protest against the staple diet of social criticism offered to playgoers. Raymond Williams, *Drama from Ibsen to Brecht* (London, 1968) and *Modern Tragedy* (London, 1966) are both useful while Ronald Gaskell looks at the different views of reality in the modern theatre in *Drama and Reality: The European Theatre Since Ibsen* (London, 1972). Michael Meyer's study *Ibsen* has been published by Penguin in 1972 in an edition abridged by the author. *Selected Plays* of W. B. Yeats, edited by A. Norman Jeffares, is published by Macmillan with a bibliography, while Yeats and his colleagues are discussed by Una Ellis-Fermor in *The Irish Dramatic Movement* (London, 1939). Allardyce Nicoll gives a history of verse dramas up to 1930 in *English Drama: 1900–1930* (Cambridge, 1973), chapter 5, part 4.

Collected Plays by Charles Williams, edited by John Heath Stubbs was published by Oxford University Press who also published the plays of Christopher Fry. The plays of Auden and Isherwood and those of T. S. Eliot are all published by Faber and Faber Ltd. T. S. Eliot is examined in D. E. Jones, *The Plays of T. S. Eliot* (London, 1960) which has a very full bibliography, and the account of how those plays came to be written and staged can be found in E. Martin Browne, *The Making of T. S. Eliot's Plays* (London 1969). Readers may also find Hugh Dickinson's *Myth on the Modern Stage* (University of Illinois, 1969) useful. Christopher Fry has attracted less attention. The British Council Pamphlet no. 54, *Christopher Fry*, by Derek Stanford, revised in 1971 has a short bibliography.

There are some short articles on the specific problems of verse and prose: Kenneth Muir, 'Verse and Prose', *Contemporary Theatre*, Stratford-upon-Avon Studies, 4, London, 1962; Katharine J. Worth, 'The Poets in the American Theatre', *American Theatre*, Stratford-upon-Avon Studies, 10, London, 1967; Dennis Welland, 'Some Post-War Experiments in Poetic Drama' and Geoffrey Bullough, 'Christopher Fry and the "Revolt" against Eliot', both printed in *Experimental Drama* (London, 1963).

In the wider context of modern theatre John Russell Brown examines the dialogue of Osborne, Arden, Wesker and Pinter in *Theatre Language* (London, 1972), and a look at plays as happening on the stage rather than between covers can be found in Raymond Williams's *Drama in Performance*, revised, extended and published as a Pelican Book in 1972. Katharine J. Worth has published an excellent study of recent British theatre, with a chapter on T. S. Eliot, called *Revolutions in Modern English Drama* (London, 1972).

For some insight into what has been happening in the theatre *The Theory of the Modern Stage* (Penguin, 1968) edited by Eric Bentley is very useful as is James Roose-Evans's *Experimental Theatre* (London, revised and extended in 1973).

And, finally, a personal look at the modern theatre by one of its poets, *the empty space* (London, 1968) by Peter Brook.

Index

Anderson, Maxwell, 28
Appia, Adolph, 12
Arden, John, 2–3, 63, 70, 72
Aristotle, 1, 2, 4
Artaud, Antonin, 12, 14, 15, 36
Auden, W. H., and Isherwood,
    Christopher, 23–7; *The Dog
    Beneath The Skin*, 23–4;
    The Ascent of F6, 24–7; *On
    The Frontier*, 27

Barnes, Peter, 74–5
Beckett, Samuel, 64–6, 68, 71
Berliner Ensemble, 69
Bottomley, Gordon, 18, 40
Brecht, Bertolt, 12, 64, 69, 71,
    72
Brook, Peter, 72, 73

Claudel, Paul, 29–30
Cocteau, Jean, 13–14, 15, 29,
    36, 44
Corneille, Pierre, 3–4
Craig, E. Gordon, 11, 12
Cummings, E. E., 27

Donoghue, Denis, *The Third
    Voice*, xi, 2, 37, 54
Duncan, Ronald, 32

Eberhart, Richard, 27
Eliot, T. S., 36, 37–52, 53, 69,
    73, 74; *The Rock*, 40–1;
    Murder in the Cathedral, 25,
    35, 37, 42–3, 45, 46; *The
    Family Reunion*, 37, 44,
    45–6; *The Cocktail Party*,
    46–9, 52; *The Confidential
    Clerk*, 37, 49–50; *The Elder
    Statesman*, 37, 50–1

Flecker, James Elroy, 17
Fry, Christopher, 53–63, 69,
    70, 73; *The Firstborn*, 55–6;
    A Phoenix Too Frequent,
    56–7; *The Lady's Not For
    Burning*, 54, 58–9; *Venus
    Observed*, 59–60; *The Dark
    Is Light Enough*, 54, 60–1;
    Curtmantle, 61; *A Yard of
    Sun*, 61–3

Giraudoux, Jean, 29, 30, 44, 69

Ibsen, Henrick, 4–10, 64
Isherwood, Christopher, *see* Auden

James, Henry, 9

La Motte, 4
Lorca, Federico Garcia, 30–1, 36
Lowell, Robert, 27

MacLeish, Archibald, 27
Masefield, John, 18
MacNeice, Louis, 28
Meiningen Players, 7, 8
Meyerhold, Vsevolod, 11, 12
Murray, J. Middleton, 17
Miller, Arthur, 58, 59; *Death of a Salesman* reviewed, 11

Noh Plays, 21, 30

Osborne, John, 69, 75

Phillips, Stephen, 16–17
Pinter, Harold, 66–7
Piscator, Erwin, 12

Shakespeare, William, 3, 39
Spender, Stephen, *Trial of a Judge*, 27
Stanislavski, Konstantin, 11
Steiner, George, *The Death of Tragedy*, xi, 3, 9, 15, 16, 44
Stevens, Wallace, 27
Storey, David, 67–8
Symons, Arthur, 12
Synge, J. M., 18, 19

Thomas, Dylan, 29
Tree, Beerbohm, 16–17

Wagner, Richard, 15
Wesker, Arnold, 69–70
Williams, Charles, 32–5
Williams, William Carlos, 27

Yeats, W. B., 8, 18, 19, 20–2, 36; *Purgatory*, 21–2